Charles Waldstein

The Work of John Ruskin

Its Influence upon modern Thought and Life

Charles Waldstein

The Work of John Ruskin
Its Influence upon modern Thought and Life

ISBN/EAN: 9783337056209

Printed in Europe, USA, Canada, Australia, Japan

Cover: Foto ©ninafisch / pixelio.de

More available books at **www.hansebooks.com**

THE WORK OF
JOHN RUSKIN

ITS INFLUENCE UPON MODERN
THOUGHT AND LIFE

BY

CHARLES WALDSTEIN

NEW YORK

HARPER AND BROTHERS
MDCCCXCIII

TO

H. F. B. L.

AND

To the Memory of

W. R. C.

CONTENTS

THE WORK OF JOHN RUSKIN

INTRODUCTION

THE claims of criticism to practical utility are not established beyond a doubt. If we run our eyes over a list of books about books, of critical reviews and commentaries on the published works of remarkable men, which every day seem to grow in bulk, we must at times have asked: " Is it not a mistake thus to block up the way between the reading public and the great books, and to occupy any portion of the small amount of time which the most studious can hardly find sufficient to devote to the reading of the great works themselves?" Even in cases where the abstruseness of the subject or the obscurity of style in the writer

1

might make some commentary accepta-
ble, it may fairly be questioned ; whether
it be **not better** for the reader **to be** forced
to make the salutary effort **at** grasping
the meaning **of** any writer (in himself
worth listening to) unaided by paraphras-
ing, **in the process** of **which much** of **the**
original author may be **lost**, while much
may be acquired from **the** transcriber,
not always **to be** considered gain ?

And as regards **the** critical review **of
the** works of great men, in which an attempt is made **at** assigning to each work
its position in the general series of similar
efforts, of throwing light **upon the origin**
and surrounding çauses of its existence
and its form, and finally of pointing **out**
what **is** good and what is bad, what is
ephemeral and what is lasting, what ought
to be confirmed and prolonged in its ex-
istence or refuted and hastened to its
descent into oblivion—in one word, the
sifting of the literary wheat from the chaff
—the utility of even this function of literary criticism may **be** questioned.   The
good and true have in themselves the
power of vitality and persistency ; while

the negative character in the bad and the untrue is the weakness at the very heart of such work, and necessarily, from its own nature, leads to annihilation. It may thus be held that *time* and the *general reading public* are the surest and fairest judges. And it is further held that no one man in one given period of time can be an adequate substitute for the judgment of the reading public in the course of ages. However many instances may be adduced in support of this doubt, careful consideration will not confirm it in its absolute form. When we come to consider what is meant by " time " and the "general reading public," instances abound in which the verdict referred to them cannot be recognized as unquestionably just. Time is a very elastic term ; and merit has been known to sleep unacknowledged for centuries, until at last it was brought into recognition by the trumpet of quickening truth and justice. We cannot help realizing that centuries are a very long time ; and it must make us shudder in our conscience when we face the possibility that there are many works

and men whose merits at the present lie
thus unrecognized, and may be so forever.*   And when we inquire how the
trumpet thus awakened them from sleep,
we find that it was sounded by one man.
In the reading public there is neither

* The duty to remember the living workers can hardly be put more eloquently than has been done by Mr.
Ruskin himself in the following passage from *Modern
Painters* (vol. i., end of chap. i.): " I do not say that this
veneration is wrong, nor that we should be less atten-
tive to the repeated words of time : but let us not forget
that if honor be for the dead, gratitude can only be for
the living.   He who has once stood beside the grave, to
look back upon the companionship which has been forever closed, feeling how impotent *there* are the wild
love, or the keen sorrow, to give one instant's pleasure to
the pulseless heart, or atone in the lowest measure to the
departed spirit for the hour of unkindness, will scarcely
for the future incur that debt to the heart, which can
only be discharged to the dust.   But the lesson which
men receive as individuals they do not learn as nations.
Again and again they have seen their noblest descend to
the grave, and have thought it enough to garland the
tombstone when they had not crowned the brow, and to
pay the honor to the ashes which they had denied to the
spirit.   Let it not displease them that they are bidden,
amid the tumult and the dazzle of their busy life, to lis-
ten for the few voices, and watch for the few lamps,
which God has toned and lighted to charm and to guide
them, that they may not learn their sweetness by their
silence, nor their light by their decay."

unity of spirit nor force of initiative; but
it, for the most part, only receives recognizable consistency in its judgment
through the leading or summarizing power of one critical writer. We must further realize that often it is one striking
fault or one palpable and salient virtue
which engrosses the attention of the readers who judge, the adherents who follow,
and the opponents who combat the whole
varied and multiform life-work of some
great man. This one feature is then sub-
stituted for the whole play of his intellectual physiognomy: for praise or for blame,
the isolation and consequent exaggeration of one side of a man's work, that may
be accidental and not essential, counteract just appreciation, or at best retard it
indefinitely. Finally, the workers themselves are not always able to indicate by
due proportion and emphasis what in
their life-work is essential and what is
accidental. When we carefully consider
and weigh all that these questions suggest, we cannot help thinking that there
is a call upon those who conscientiously
feel themselves qualified for the task, to

lead or to direct the judgment of the reading public, and to interfere with the course of fatalistic and indifferent time.

Still graver doubts may be felt as regards the propriety or advisability of dealing critically with the work of a living man. Good taste, on the one hand, is in danger of being affected by the personal character which might be assumed by contemporary criticism; while, on the other hand, the claim of time might be still more strongly urged as a necessary agent in giving due proportion to merit and influence. Yet even here we feel that historical fatalism and intellectual *laissez faire* may retard the certainty of progress. It will, in every case, greatly depend upon the amount of obvious importance which such work actually has before we determine whether it is desirable to fix and to confirm its existence by insisting upon what is good and by pointing out what is not. If only criticism is not personal, but dispassionate and sincere, it can but lead to a strengthening and a support of good work. The price of immortality is contemporary criticism.

This is the spirit in which the writer proposes to approach his subject, which (considering the general spread of a desire for artistic education, and the important position which in this respect Mr. Ruskin has held, holds, and will hold) appears worthy of critical treatment in the present day.

In dealing with John Ruskin at all, we must, from the very outset, be aware that we are dealing with a striking personality and with a great life-work. To sum these up positively and shortly, we should say that the central feature of the greatness of the personality consists in the bold instance he presents of a man who has dared to *live* his thoughts. And if we should feel that there are inconsistencies in his life, these do not arise from the usual cause of such inconsistency, namely, the discrepancy or contradiction between practice and profession, between the actual course and the theory of life: when mystical, ascetic, and other-worldly

preachers shine in the ball-room and spec-
ulate on the stock-exchange; when philosophers, historians, and scients, whose
vision penetrates down to the principles
of all things, soars over countless ages
in the history of nations, and traces the
links that bind things animate and inanimate together, crouch before an ephemeral prejudice or fashion of a petty lo-
cality; and when economists and social
reformers pen the gospel of socialism over
oysters and champagne. If Ruskin's life
appears inconsistent, the contradictions
are to be sought for in his thoughts and
theories.

The positive aspect of his work, and
the debt which England, and through it
the civilized world, owes to him, might
be summed up in the following survey:

The great change which appears to
have been effected in the history of contemporary civilization in England during
the generation preceding our own is to be
found mainly in the diffusion of culture,
or at least of a desire and need for it,
among the mass of the middle and lower
classes, owing to changes in the condi-

tions of these classes, physical, political, and social, which in their previous state maintained the aristocratic constitution of British society. Culture, in its refined form, was in England the possession of one section of the nobility and of the higher professional and literary classes; and its possession was here more exclusively confined to this limited group than in any other of the occidental countries of Europe. The other sections of the community, as well as those members of the nobility and gentry in the country who were addicted chiefly to field sports, or whose means did not permit of the acquisition of a library and of frequent visits to the metropolis, as well as the bulk of the merchant class and the tradesmen, whose type Dickens has fixed, only possessed for the satisfaction and sustenance of their spiritual and intellectual life of higher emotions the ministrations and usages of the Church. And the higher educational institutions, such as the universities, which in Germany, together with the national theatres, developed the secular side of moral life and supplemented the religious education from their completely emancipated position, were in England, if not quite an ancillary appendage to the Church, at least directly subject to **her** influence. **While, on** the one hand, this absorption on the part of the Church of the higher side of moral and artistic life, and the exclusive sway which she exercised **for** centuries, have retarded the domestication of these independent forms of civilization as such, she has, on the other hand, in her modified **form,** nurtured these needs **in** the hearts of the people. We must, for instance, recognize that the Puritanic wave, which might have completely submerged and dissipated the current of popular music among what I venture to consider a naturally musical people, **was to a certain** degree arrested **in its** destructive advance by the opportunities which the Church offered for the continuous study and progressive flow of English church music. Thus, while popular and secular music have continuously degenerated, and have been repressed into the shallow regions **of** vulgarity and false sentiment, to

our present **day of** a promising revival,
the compositions of English church music
manifested an unbroken strong vitality,
in which not even the tyrannical and **ex-**
clusive reign of the giant Handel could
quite extirpate a native characteristic
force. At the same time, furthermore,
under its protection, with **all** classes **of**
Englishmen the appreciation for music
(though narrow) has been fostered, and
the ability to sing intelligently has been
given to vast numbers in whom otherwise such an accomplishment would not
have been expected. The same may apply to the interest in architecture, which
appears to me to be more wide-spread in
an intelligent form among all **classes of**
Englishmen than in any other country.
While it is thus undoubtedly the case,
that the Church in England **has** been,
and is still for the greater part of its pop-
ulation, the only means of sustaining or
reviving **the** higher needs of culture and
of providing **a** flower-garden amid the
endless monotony **of** fields for the **pro-**
duction of bread - stuff and moors for
grouse - shooting, the fact remains **that,**

owing chiefly to her influence, the classes
referred to have been and are still, in
their intellectual education, in the variety
and diversity of their moral resources,
and in their appreciativeness of the prod-
ucts of literature, science, and art, far below the *bourgeoisie* of Germany. Within the last decades a marked change has
taken place in this respect. The middle
classes in the country and in the towns,
and even large portions of the laboring
classes, have in every direction manifested their desire for the acquisition of
the higher fruits of culture, and have
made heard their claim to share in the
birthright which previously had been as-
signed but to the few. Nay, the strength
of the movement has been so great, its
impetus has been so powerful and rapid,
that, as is so often the case, it may tem-
porarily have overshot its proper mark,
and landed in the district that lies beyond the boundaries of sincerity and
moderation, the sphere of the grotesque
and ridiculous. Yet we may venture upon
the paradox that no movement is really
progressing unless it can occasionally be

laughed **at,** that no social or political innovation can be made, unless the rapid
ity of its advance has been occasionally
checked in a salutary degree by the powerful pages of that important teacher
Punch. Amid the numerous causes which
might be adduced for the consummation
of this great change in English life, the
direct efforts of individual men must be
noted, and among these I hold that **no**
two men have been as efficient in their
work as Matthew Arnold and Ruskin.
Of the nature of Mr. Ruskin's work in
this direction, of its faults, and at the
same time its peculiar effectiveness, I
shall treat **in the** succeeding portions **of**
this essay.

Another distinctive characteristic marking the life of the English people in the
present day is the growing feeling of economical responsibility. It manifests itself
in the extension of the laws of morality,
which **had** hitherto, as it were, been only
valid for and applicable to the domestic
life, or the life **of** disinterested social intercourse, **to** the spheres of economical
life. And this movement has penetrated

into the body of economical theory itself,
and has made those views of writers on
this subject, **who but a** short time ago
put economy and ethics as absolutely distinct if not opposed spheres, appear **completely** antiquated. But though the inner
development of economical study and the
reaction against the Manchester school
may have contributed to this salutary
change in economical doctrine, the change
is not entirely the outcome of theoretical
study, but has mainly been caused by the
final introduction into theory of what
practically has been a constant growth in
the moral organization **of** social life in
England. Here again the causes for this
change have been numerous and varied,
but the efforts of individuals can be discerned ; and among **them we may (in**
spite of some of his economical theories)
point **to** the spirit **in** the work of Mill
himself, to the influence of Kingsley and
Maurice, to the works of George Eliot,
and to the main spirit of the preaching
of Ruskin.

As he has been a contributor to the
general advance in the intellectual and

social life of England, he has **to a** still higher degree been an active factor in producing a change in the more special sphere of art. It is here that he of **all** men has been **the** most prominent in bringing about a diffusion of the taste for art among the classes previously referred to, and that he has greatly elevated the standing of the profession of an artist itself. On the one hand **we must** consider (judging from past personal experience, or present inference based upon the study of the picture the literary records **give us,** and the extant traces and survivals) the dryness and joylessness of the domestic life among the greater number of the English people fifty years ago, the vulgarity of **taste,** the meanness **or taw-** driness of domestic architecture and decoration, the wanton ravages and destruction of the great monuments of man's life and artistic efforts in past ages. On the other hand we must become aware of the fact that now, at least the desire for artistic decoration (not always rightly guided), for the adornment of houses, for the preservation of artistic remains,

has penetrated through all classes; that
the homes of the merchant, the tradesman, the city clerk, and even the artisan,
all make some pretence and manifest
some desire towards the raising of their
tastes, and the consequent embellishment
of their surroundings; that even the athletic undergraduate haunts the curiosity-
shop; that not only the Academy exhibi-
tion in London but those of provincial
towns form an important staple of conversation (not always judicious or even
sincere) for so large a portion of the community. When we compare these facts we
cannot help but realize the great change
that has come over English life. And
this, again, is in great part due to the efforts of John Ruskin, and of some other
workers, like William Morris.

Ruskin has done much in raising the
appreciation of art in general, more especially the art of painting, most in bringing into proper prominence the department of landscape - painting. This department was not appreciated sufficiently,
and even now is not valued enough by
the greater number of people, as compared

.

with third-rate works of historical and of *genre* painting.

It is difficult to estimate how much Ruskin has done directly for the artists themselves in the pursuit of their vocation. But there can be no doubt that he has powerfully impressed upon them the seriousness and responsibility of their life-work, and has raised their enthusiasm; that he has done much to deepen and elevate the general tone prevailing among them, which often, among the followers of that high craft, tends towards social dissonance. He has waged relentless warfare against the fetich of false genius erected on the central height of the international country of Bohemia. He has opposed the fatal superstition that the positive power of artistic inventiveness was increased and intensified by an unsocial indulgence, by a life that differed in its appearance and in its laws of conduct from those that hold good for all members of a well-organized society possessed of dignity — the superstition which caused a second-rate painter to taunt the simple violin-maker Stradivarius with the com-

2

parison of their pursuits—in mouthing
that

"higher arts
Subsist on freedom—eccentricity—
Uncounted inspirations—influence
That comes with drinking, gambling, talk turned wild,
Then moody misery and lack of food—
With every dithyrambic fine excess:
These make at last a storm which flashes out
In lightning revelations. Steady work
Turns genius to a loom; the soul must lie
Like grapes beneath the sun till ripeness comes
And mellow vintage."

He has thus contributed his share in
giving to the painter of England the
somewhat exceptional social position
which he holds, owing to the general estimate the public has of his profession,
which makes him a highly respected member of the community.

A further great merit of Ruskin, and
one for which the world cannot be sufficiently grateful to him, is found in the
fact that he has opened out to many, who
would otherwise not have been possessed
of it, the appreciation of Turner. It may
perhaps be wrong to suppose that the
merits of Turner were unrecognized when
Ruskin wrote his brilliant defence of him.

That this could not have been entirely the case is perhaps borne out by the simple fact of the material success he had as a painter, coupled with the exceptionally early age at which he was admitted into the body of the Royal Academicians, and the two hundred and forty paintings he exhibited on the walls of the Royal Academy. Still the fact remains that the newness and boldness of the departure in landscape-painting did not, and does not always even now, make him easily accessible to the greater number of people whose standards of taste are based upon and developed by the canons of art contained in the landscapes of previous masters, and who are not in the habit of carefully and lovingly observing nature in her broad features and in her varied changes. Yet, I hold that no man, not even he who is by nature and circumstance prepared to appreciate works of art, and in the habit of so doing, can approach the works of Turner after he has read Ruskin without having his perceptive sense quickened, so that new beauties and truths are manifest to him that were before hidden.

And this faculty of appreciating Turner, which becomes a lesson in the more careful observation of all landscape-painting —nay, all pictures and works of art—has been strengthened and widened by Ruskin in the guidance which he gives for a revived and intensified observation of nature herself in a new spirit and with a new method.

It is here that I believe Ruskin's greatest achievement is to be found, and one with which his name will ever have to be associated. He has endowed man with a new habit of mind, and has laid the foundation for a new class of observation, which I believe to be midway between science and art, or rather overlapping into both. I shall call this new intellectual discipline Phænomenology of Nature. It is the summing-up of a scale of effort beginning with Byron, passing through Shelley and Wordsworth, and leading to Ruskin, strongly modified and directed, on the one hand, by the predominant wave of observation in modern natural science, and, on the other hand, by the development of landscape-painting,

especially since Turner. I do not mean
that in Ruskin the ultimate consummation of this method of observing nature
has been reached ; on the contrary, I consider his merit to consist in the founding
of it. But I believe that the promises it
gives, if pursued in the course he has in-
dicated, while perhaps it may never be
accompanied by the power and beauty of
his eloquence of exposition, has not been
fully realized by those who have considered it purely from the point of view of
art or purely of science.

This power of eloquence and expression
brings us to the last point, in which the
undoubted virtue of Ruskin will always
call for the gratitude of the English-speak-
ing nations. He appears to me the greatest of English prose poets. And if his
writing be criticised as prose for its being
too much like poetry, and as poetry for
evading its definite forms in being clad in
the apparel of prose, this merely means,
as has ever been the case, that our cri-
teria of what is admissible or praise-
worthy are too narrow or not sufficiently
numerous, that new tests will have to be

applied to new things, and that those whose tastes have been formed exclusively on old standards, will have to enlarge their sympathies and to adapt themselves to the new objects they would appreciate or judge.

These are, to my mind, the main positive deeds and works for which the world is indebted to Ruskin, and, as such, they have the power of prevailing, and it is to be hoped will be justly recognized. I have here singled out what I consider to be the main features of the good he has done, and I have not attempted to weigh accurately the influence which his work has had and may have upon contemporary life and thought. To do this at all adequately requires a fuller critical examination, which, from its difficulty, must call forth the diffidence of him who undertakes it. There is hardly a figure in the history of contemporary thought in England the intellectual and social influence of which it is so difficult to gauge as that of John Ruskin. This difficulty is owing to the complex nature of his work and of his personality. With the latter we are only concerned in so far as it throws light upon the work, as the knowledge of it is merely derived indirectly from the character of his work, or more directly in what he himself has permitted us to see in his published confessions, and in so far as through his work, or in connection with it, it influenced men.

The difficulty of forming a just estimate of the influence of Mr. Ruskin, owing to the complexity of his work, is to be found, first, in the variety of subjects with which he has dealt, ranging over most of the important spheres that actuate human life ; secondly, in the fact that, within this width of range, the marked distinction which generally serves to classify intellectual workers into two broad groups, namely, the practical and theoretical, does not hold good in his case. For his activity lays claim to both spheres. And the complication is increased by the fact that, when he himself claims to be theoretical or scientific (and in the superficial appearance of it is so), there is an actual predominance of the practical or ethical aim, not only as the immediate motive **and** ultimate goal of his endeavor, but constantly interfilleted and interwoven with the theoretical tissue, and often interfering with and confusing its consistency, and diminishing or destroying its unity of structure and effective service. On the other hand, the manifestly practical works often suffer **from** an apparent and obtrusive predominance of preconceived **general** maxims, resting upon foundations the materials for which seem **to** be drawn **out of the** domain of pure theory, and **thus** have not upon them **the** impress of the sympathetic observa**tion** of practical life. In addition to these broader recognizable causes of complexity, there are, in each separate department and individual instance of his work, similar intricacies and **often** confusions in **the** detailed elaboration **of** tasks and problems, which at times **make** any attempt **at a** just appreciation of the work (not **to** speak of **an** estimate of **its** influence) appear almost hopeless. **There is** much that is good absolutely ; still more that is **good when** severed from its general **con-**

text; more still that is admirable when considered as an individual flash of inspiration or thought or description; and much that is bad, merely because of the false position in which it is put; even some things that are bad absolutely. And, throughout, the student or sympathetic reader (and the two ought to be synonymous) feels that he ought constantly to shift his position and alter his focus in viewing and considering the connected portions of any given work, looking upon a part as a piece of sober criticism and philosophy, while the apparent next link in the chain ought, if real justice were done it, to be considered a painting transcribed into words, or a poem, or a portion of a sermon, or a fairy tale. And one must feel that true justice would only be done to the works of Ruskin if, with infinite labor, some sympathetic and congenial spirit, possessed of much sobriety and system, were to rearrange the whole of the works, and to distribute passages taken from them all under new heads, with a simple, intelligible, and orderly classification.

In attempting to estimate Ruskin's influence, we must needs be critical of his work. Nor do I in any way propose, even if I were fitted for it, to attempt the task of reorganization suggested above. But for our purpose it is necessary to view the man and his work under several heads.

First, then, I shall consider Ruskin as a writer on art; second, as the founder of the phænomenology of nature; third, as a writer and prose poet; fourth, as a writer on social, political, and economical questions; and finally, I shall endeavor to give a summary of the influence of his work and of the example of his life, as he has made them manifest to the public.

I

RUSKIN AS A WRITER ON ART

RUSKIN'S strongest points and greatest achievements are not, I maintain, to be found in the domain of the theory and criticism of art. Though he has shown himself to be possessed of the most refined power of observation and appreciation of even hidden beauties, I believe that this appreciation and refinement of taste are directed, on the one hand, more to nature, on the other, more to the ethical world; and that art as such does not respond to the natural bent of his mind. He is primarily a lover and minute observer of nature and a moral preacher; and the predominance of these two attitudes of mind often stands in the way of the right understanding of art. Before we begin to consider Ruskin's general theory of art, I must point to two acci-

dental impediments which would increase
the difficulty of his constructing a sound
theory of art. The one is to be found in
the accepted common meaning or deno-
tation of the term art in England; the
other, in the accidental origin and restricted purpose of Ruskin's first general
book on art, perhaps his greatest work,
namely, *Modern Painters*.

Many people in England, when they
speak of art, merely have in their minds
paintings and painters, many include
sculpture, many architecture; but few go
beyond this. It is perhaps due to the
concrete and inductive spirit of the English people, which has also manifested
itself, I believe harmfully, in the restricted use of the term science in ordinary
parlance, commonly used as synonymous
and coextensive with natural science, including, perhaps, the so-called exact sciences. That art includes not only the
formative arts, such as painting, sculpture, and architecture, but also all forms
of music and poetry, down to the very
novel—in fact all man's work so far as
it is directly meant to produce æsthetic

pleasure—is not present to the minds of most people when they use the term. At all events, the predominance which is given to painting in any consideration of art is very marked, and this general use of the term, which has not been effectively altered by those who have written on the theory of art, has limited and narrowed and often distorted the range of vision of critics, and has vitiated the soundness of general theory at the very first approach to the main problems.

The accidental fact that Ruskin's general and most fundamental work on art dealt predominantly, not only with painting, but chiefly with one side of painting, and that it had a fixed immediate apologetic aim of vindicating the right, not only of modern painters in general as opposed to their classic predecessors, but of one great modern painter in especial, Turner, has, I believe, hampered him in his general views on art ever after, even f, by disposition and training, he had been more fitted to solve with the sublime sobriety of well-balanced, systematic thought the great problems of æsthetics.

The first fact which he who would attempt to elaborate a systematic theory of art must constantly bear in mind is that he is' dealing with the theory of art, and not with art itself; that he is aiming at the complete and systematic apprehension of facts which are to satisfy the need and craving for truth, and not with the creation of that which is to produce æsthetic pleasure and satisfy man's need for beauty. The confusion of the spirit in which we are to approach the theory of a pursuit with the spirit of the pursuit itself is most easily made and most fatal in its results. In other words, the temptation is always great on the part of the art theorist or critic (and the expectant attitude of the public with regard to his work increases this danger) to cast aside the measured sobriety of analysis required for criticism and the establishment of theory the moment the subject with which he is dealing happens to partake of the emotional nature of artistic creation. It must be confessed that the attitude of mind of a writer on the theory and criticism of art is no more that of a painter, poet, or musician than that of a historian carefully sifting his facts from all available records is that of a general fighting a battle, or than that of a zoologist studying the nature and development of animal form is that of a breeder of cattle. Yet the main attitude of mind actuating the writer on the theory of art is to be the same as that of the sound historian or biologist, however different the objects with which they deal may be among each other, and he must equally guard—nay, from the nature of his subject, must be more on his guard—against the easy insinuation of alien interests and tempting forms of inaccurate diction. He must study carefully and minutely the nature of man's æsthetic feelings and the causes which produce them, and must consider with equal thoroughness the common features of man's works whose chief purpose it is to appeal to these feelings. He may have to ask himself whether there are any universally accepted and intelligible causes for these feelings, whether art and the beautiful are not purely a matter of more or less individual taste or opinion, whether æsthetics is not purely what Plato called δόξα, or whether there is any universally admitted ground for it, making it what Plato would call ἐπιστήμη. Then, having ascertained that art does not rest upon mere individual taste and opinion, but is grounded upon the fundamental constitution of man's senses and emotion and intellect, in their normal and sane development, **he** must set to work, **by** a very wide but none the less careful **and** exhaustive analysis, induction, and **even** experiment, to examine man's nat**ure** and his **work in** their relation to harmony, **beauty,** or art ; and he must, above **all,** always hold before his eyes **the su**preme aim, upon which all his **powers** ought to be jealously concentrated, **of ar**riving at the truth, **and nothing but the·** truth, independent of all other or further considerations. **This will in** itself be a high moral act, pleasing to God.

Now it is in this necessary, fundamental, and leading attitude of mind that Ruskin fails, from the very outset, in dealing with the theory of art ; and the radiation from this false centre **of vision has put** out of focus many of the points with which he deals in detail.

According to him all art is revelation and all art is praise. This at once **gives** a religious bias to **scientific** investigation. I call it bias, because considerations that might be introduced ultimately, when the main facts have been established, are here prematurely presented, thus fatally retarding and distorting the just apprehension of the facts themselves. **From a** purely religious point of view all actions may be and ought to be viewed in their relation to eternity, to the wholeness of **the** universe, and to God; and it may be right, for some habitually, and for others occasionally, to dwell upon and to ponder over this higher interrelation **of things** and acts. But this is **none** the truer of art than it is of science or politics, or even **of** the acquisition of wealth. Yet our **progress would** surely **be** retarded if we distracted **our** attention **from the** individual thing we were doing, and directed it towards **the** ethical, metaphysical, **or** theological **considerations of its possible** ultimate bearings. The task, **in** itself arduous, of the scientific apprehension of relations that subsist, or that may exist, between a **complicated variety of** things, is, to **say the** least, not furth**ered** by the introduction of that which **is still remoter,** more incomprehensible, and incapable of demonstrable test. And we must, above **all,** be ever mindful of the fact that **the** insinuating obtrusiveness **of the** *personal equation* is more **likely to** assert itself successfully in these remote and ultimate regions of thought than in the nearer and more familiar fields of pure scientific in-**quiry.** The solution of the main **prob-**lems **of** art is as little advanced by the introduction of theological considerations as the cause of biology or chemistry would be furthered by it. George **Eliot's** violin-maker, **in the pride of his humble craft, was** fully conscious of the godliness of his **good work** when he said :

> " My work is mine,
> **And,** heresy **or not, if my** hand slacked
> **I** should rob God—since He **is** fullest good—
> Leaving a blank instead of violins.
> I say, not God himself **can make man's best**
> Without **best men to help Him.** I am **one best**
> Here **in** Cremona, **using** sunlight well

To fashion finest maple till it serves
More cunningly than throats for harmony.
'Tis rare delight: I would not change my skill
To be the Emperor with bungling hands,
And lose my work, which comes as natural
As self at waking."

But, on the other hand, he knew that whatever his hand found to do he was to do it with his might, and not to dissipate his strength by looking for praise or revelation; and as the aim of his art was to make the best violins from the point of view of violin-making, or, at most, violin-playing, the praise was contained in the good violins as violins, and not in any way as indirect and obscure sermons or songs.

"And as my stomach, so my eye and hand,
And inward sense that works along with both,
Have hunger that can never feed on coin.
Who draws a line and satisfies his soul,
Making it crooked where it should be straight?
An idiot with an oyster-shell may draw
His lines along the sand all wavering,
Fixing no point or pathway to a point;
An idiot one remove may choose his line,
Straggle and be content; but God be praised
Antonio Stradivari has an eye
That winces at false work and loves the true,

With hand and **arm** that play upon the tool
As willingly as any singing bird
Sets him **to sing his** morning roundelay,
Because he **likes to sing and likes the** song."

I therefore say that Ruskin prematurely introduces religious and ethical **considerations,** and in dealing with the theory of **art he** does not direct all **his concentrated** forces towards the answering of the question " what is **true?"** but **"what is holy," or** " good," or " good for," or **better,"** or " worse ?"

The results of this make themselves **felt** from the very outset. He will not go dispassionately to the foundation of human feelings and the earliest and simplest sensations of man, not only in his highest state of civilization, but **in his crudest** stage **of** intellectual development. **He** appears to dwell **with reluctance** upon the nature of sensation, **and he** dislikes the very term itself, substituting *theoria* for *aisthesis.* For him the early sensations **are** not the simple fundamental factors with which the theorist has to deal **dispassionately; but they** are viewed **in the** light of the moral **teacher to whom they**

are the lower as compared with the higher
thoughts and feelings, which latter often
really are mystical and fanciful rhapso-
dies. His fundamental and introductory
chapters on the theory of art, in Part III.
of the second volume of *Modern Painters*,
are either rhetorical (often very beautiful)
preachings, or attempts at defining "the
distinctions of *dignity* among pleasures
of sense." The really fundamental questions concerning the nature of our sense-
perceptions in their relation to our feelings of form and beauty he slurs over
hastily in a few pages, and then takes up
his favorite strain in dealing with "the
temper by which right taste is formed,"
rather than with the real question, what
right taste is or ought to be. It surely
brings us no further to say that "we may
indeed perceive, as far as we are acquainted with the nature of God, that we have
been so constructed as in a healthy state
of mind to derive pleasure from whatever
things are illustrative of that nature." If
he could undertake soberly and adequately to define the nature of God, we might
then test the healthy state of man's mind

by it. But this **he** does not do. In the
same chapter (Book **II.**, chap. iii.) he brings
the problem to **a point** : " Hence there
arise two questions, according to the sense
in which the word right **is taken—the first,**
in what **way an** impression of sense **may**
be deceptive, and therefore a conclusion
respecting it untrue ; and the second, **in**
what way an impression of sense, or **the**
preference of **one, may be** a subject of
will, and therefore of moral duty or delin-
quency." To the first **of** these (a really
fundamental one) he devotes a short paragraph, referring **us** to " the common con-
sent of man " (which man, or men, or race,
or age ?). But the second question **ad-**
mits of preaching, and he **dwells upon it**
with fervent eloquence.

This religious bias manifests itself **fur-**
thermore in the mystical tendency apparent in his headings and subdivisions. Take,
for instance, his types of beauty : "Infinity, or the Type of Divine Incomprehensi-
bility ; **Unity,** the Type of Divine Compre-
hensiveness ; Repose, the Type of Divine
Permanence ; Symmetry, the Type of **Di-**
vine **Justice ;** Purity, **the type of Divine**

Energy" (why not Divine Purity?); "Moderation, the Type of Government by Law." This mystical admixture vitiates the character of his *Seven Lamps of Architecture*, in which much is said of real value, while in the " Lamp of Sacrifice," forming the first chapter, it leads him to the most absurd jugglery, from the artistic and historical point of view. Nay, we cannot help feeling that, even from a theological point of view, his formalistic mysticism has often led him away from the moderation of good taste into serio - comic niceties which remind us of one of the class of injudicious preachers who thought he had found a good example of gratitude in the brute creation when he referred to the duck that looks up to thank its Maker when drinking water, whereas this involuntary movement depends entirely upon the formation of its throat. But it makes itself felt in its disturbing influence even in his definite estimate of technical aspects of landscape - painting, as, for instance, the importance he attaches to luminous backgrounds of pictures as suggestive or expressive of infinity. This leads him to say (*Modern Painters*, II., chap. v.) that he knows "not any truly great painter of any time who manifests not the most intense pleasure in the luminous space of his backgrounds, or who ever sacrifices this pleasure where the nature of his subject admits of its attainment, as, on the other hand, I know not that the habitual use of dark backgrounds can be shown as having ever been consistent with pure and high feeling, and, except in the case of Rembrandt (and then under peculiar circumstances only), with any high power of intellect."

It is owing to this theory of art as a revelation that I believe Ruskin has formulated his own theory with regard to the relation between art and nature; though, perhaps, the zeal with which he defended Turner against the charge of violating in his paintings truth to nature, which gave a stimulus to his first effort in his art writings, may have had some influence in thus fixing his views. To Ruskin the function of art is to be the intermediator between man and nature, or rather is to reveal to man the divine spirit in nature.

The great artist is he who can thus perceive **most** fully this divine **spirit** which pervades the world, and who has the power **of** reproducing adequately the **revelation** thus made to him, and of enabling other **denser souls to be** pervaded **with,** and illumined by, **this** heaven-born light.

It is exceedingly difficult to ascertain exactly what is Ruskin's theory of the relation of **art to** nature. **It** would be easy to show that he holds different views at different times, continually contradicting **one another.** But I believe it would be **fairest to him and** to **his work to** put in simple terms what I consider his principal view, and **the one most in** keeping with the best he has said on other topics.

To him nature **is** pervaded **with** the divine spirit, and there is no evil in her. **He** is distinctly teleological. There is, **he** believes, always a divine spirit in nature, **provided** only we **do** not interfere with her, and, as artists, have the **power of discerning it. Now** the true artist **is he who** can thus **perceive** the divine element in nature most fully, **and** his function **is to** enable others, by means of his work, **to**

perceive this spirit, which otherwise they
could not apprehend. The artist is most
likely to fulfil this supreme function if
he studies nature simply, earnestly, and
truthfully, reproduces adequately what he
thus sees, and does not cast the "dark
shadow of himself and his personality
over her," attempting "to improve upon
nature."

Now, even granting his teleological
premise that all nature is pervaded with
this divine spirit, which is ever good and
beautiful, and that the supreme task rests
with the artist in discerning and reproducing it, we are then but at the beginning
of the whole problem of art and its relation to nature. For the different artists,
in search of this divine spirit, will see it
in different parts and lights and aspects,
according to their personal, moral, intellectual, or artistic characters; and even
the same artist will see a different spirit
in the same scene in his varying moods,
or under the different aspects which he
chooses to accentuate. A Titian, a Rembrandt, a Turner, a J. F. Millet, may all
have believed, or claimed, to have seized

the divine revelation in the nature they reproduced. But surely the spirit of the work lay in this personal element which they added or infused, the unity of soul which welded together into a necessary whole the infinite multiplicity of phenomena before them and the innumerable possibilities of scenes to be reproduced. What makes it art is this human organization of the facts of nature. Or may not this be considered the really *divine* element, breathed by God through man's best effort into inanimate or insentient nature?

Ruskin and many others have made the mistake of attempting to solve the fundamental principle of all art in dealing with painting or with any *imitative* art. Ruskin himself (*Modern Painters*, II., chap. i.) has once stated that architecture is not so pure an art as sculpture and painting, because of the alien considerations of construction and utility mixing with the "theoretic" or æsthetic side of art. On similar grounds I maintain that, for the discovery of the principles of all art, those arts which reproduce known

forms of nature, such as sculpture and
painting, and must thus appeal fully and
powerfully to man's sense of truthful apprehension and comparison before they
can act upon or satisfy his sense of form
and harmony, are not so likely to yield
satisfactory results as the more purely
decorative arts and the early forms of
music, and are not so clearly expressive
of man's artistic instinct. But to this
sober, and on the face of it humble, point
of departure Ruskin's impetuous or impatient flights of inspiration and enthusias-
tic rhetoric will not descend. To ascertain the fundamental principle of art, we
proceed more safely the less the art is
imitative, and appeals to truth as well as
beauty, or to beauty through truth. I do
not mean to say that art ends there; on
the contrary, it rises and grows more
complex, appealing to all the highest
thoughts and aspirations as it mixes with
truth and goodness. But for the discovery of its fundamental principles, the early
traces of man's creative artistic efforts—
nay, their origin in the constitution of
the human senses—are the only safe field

of investigation. It is only as these are studied dispassionately and thoroughly that we arrive at the true principles underlying our highest artistic experiences.

Ruskin is thus necessarily not quite clear in his conception of the distinction between art and science when he illustrates their difference in saying that "science informs us that the sun is ninety-five millions of miles distant from and one hundred and eleven times broader than the earth, that we and all the planets revolve round it, and that it revolves on its own axis in twenty-five days, fourteen hours, and four minutes. With all this art has nothing whatever to do. It has no care to know anything of this kind. But the things which it does care to know are these: that in the heavens God has set a tabernacle for the sun, which is as a bridegroom coming out of his chamber, and rejoiceth as a strong man to run a race. His going forth is from the end of the heaven, and his circuit unto the ends of it; and there is nothing hid from the heat thereof." Art, according to him, does not only deal with truths of aspect,

but its main function is to discover truths
of essence, and hence it is much vaster in
its field and scope, as the soul is larger
than the material creation. This is fair
neither to science nor to art. Science *is*
chiefly concerned with the truths of essence, the inner constitution, causes of
change, origin, future destiny of objects
that lie below what can actually be per-
ceived by the senses. Above all, the
causes of existence and change are the
true province of science. Art, on the
other hand, does, above all, deal with the
form and aspect of things; and there is a
soul and spirit to be found in this æsthetic side of things, as it is to be found in
their scientific, philosophical, ethical, and
religious side.

This being Ruskin's conception of the
relation between art and nature, we can
quite understand how he sets as the supreme task of the artist the realization
of truth ; and though he widens out the
term truth to comprehend much that
would ordinarily be summarized under a
different head, still he is enabled often to
go to the very root of things, and to de-

stroy many superstitions and fallacies
that have prevailed in criticism, and that
have misdirected practice. Still, the fact
remains that the ultimate aim of science
is truth, the ultimate aim of art is the
production of æsthetic pleasures by means
of what we must at present call harmony
or beauty. This harmony, corresponding
to a fundamental need and longing for
design and order in the human mind,
rooted in the nature and development of
man's simplest sensations, and growing
and flowering into his highest spiritual
aspirations, man wishes to project into
nature, and to realize in the confused web
of the multitudinous disordered events
in life that crowd in upon his attention.
In his artistic efforts he is thus driven to
select, rearrange, or compose things and
facts in nature in accordance with the
need of this essential quality of his own
mind. But we can quite well understand
how Ruskin is strongly opposed to this
view of its being the function of art to
select, or, as he would call it, to improve
upon nature ; and it is one of the leading
features of his personality, no doubt influ-

encing also his social and political views,
that he has a sacred horror of the act of
man's hand in defiling nature as she is.
Still, as regards art, it would be nearer
the truth to say that man's artistic efforts
have their origin in his opposition to nature than in his following her, though
both would be overstated. But should
Ruskin's view of the position of truth in
art hold good, however he may choose
to define truth, the necessary and consistent consequence would lead him to minute and accurate photographic reproduction as the highest consummation of art,
however much he would be the first to
shrink from and condemn such a result.
He would certainly be astonished to find
that the same fundamental principles are
adopted by Zola, and have served him as
the theoretical justification of the aber-
rations in his work. Zola makes his author speak with a fervor and a largeness
of vision and power of diction which do
justice to that view. "No, no ; they do
not know ; they ought to know. . . . I,
every time that a professor tried to force
truth upon me, felt the opposition of mis-

trust in thinking, ' He is mistaken, or is misleading me.' Their ideas exasperate me ; it appears to me that truth is wider than all that. . . . Ah ! how beautiful it would be to give one's whole existence to a work in which one would endeavor to put things and animals and man, the immense arc, not in the order of the philosophical manuals, according to the stupid hierarchy in which our pride cradles itself, but in the full flow of universal life, a world in which we should only be an accident, where the dog that passes, nay, down to the stone on the road-side, would supplement and explain our existence, in short, the great all, without high or low, without soiled or clean, just as it lives and has its function ! . . . Surely to science the novelists and poets must turn ; she is to-day the only possible source. Ah ! but what are we to take from her, how walk beside her ? I immediately feel that I flounder. . . . Ah ! if I knew how, if I knew how, what a series of books I should fling at the head of the mob !" Yes, indeed, if one knew how to deal with truths. But here begins the whole task

4

of art. And he makes his truth-loving
painter say: "Ah! life, life! To feel her
give herself in her reality, to love her for
her own sake, eternal and ever changing,
not to have the foolish idea of ennobling
her in enfeebling her, to realize that the
would-be uglinesses are only juttingsforth
of character, and to cause to live, and to
make men, the only way of being a
god!"

Be all this as it may, with regard to
Ruskin's general theory and much of its
application, the fact remains that in his
chapters on truth he has succeeded in
setting a new standard in many departments of what with a barbarous word we
might call the typology of nature. He
has shown for all times, for instance, that
man and animals and costumes and buildings are not the only subjects which deserve careful observation and adequate
rendering by the painter, but that the
configuration of the soil, and the profile
of mountains, and the different trees and
shrubs and flowers, nay, leaves and twigs,
have all a distinct character that has a
claim upon our careful attention, and

ought to be adequately rendered, and not caricatured, in a painting.

He justly calls our attention to the fact that we all turn in indignation from a painter who draws a horse, even in the background of his picture, so that we might mistake it for a man or a cow or a rock, while in many much-admired pictures by old masters trees and rocks have not only been robbed of their individuality, but endowed with a monstrous compound character made up of the unintelligible confusion of traits belonging to different bodies. We must feel that the more the observing power of the public grows in this direction, fostered by the higher standards of truth in the landscape-painters, or forcing them to raise their standard, the higher will the art of landscape-painting grow in this direction, not only with regard to correct drawing, but also with regard to the treatment of light and shade and color, freeing these from the restricting bondage of a uniform studio light.

The introduction of the elements which thus disturb the purely scientific spirit of

his inquiry (all of which may be summed
up in the phrase, the intrusion of the personal equation) has also diminished the
value of Ruskin as a historian of art. In
fact it is here that his range of sympathies is particularly narrow — narrowed
by those views of personal predilection
which he himself would suppose were directed by his general ruling passion for
moral and religious principles. But even
if we admit the justness of the introduction of these considerations into the sober
work of a true historian, it remains possible and even probable that many false
steps will be made in the application of
these moral and religious tenets to the remote facts of past history (in themselves
difficult to apprehend in truth and clearness); and it appears to me, for instance,
to require a great deal of imaginative skill
to summarize much of Venetian history
and art under definite moral heads, even
if the facts were clearer than they really
are. I venture to believe that in his deal-
ings with history, as well as with art, he
has unconsciously, owing to these preconceived unscientific interests and motives,

clipped and arranged and forced facts into a grouping for which these facts had not the remotest natural predisposition or elective affinity. This unhistoric and unscientific prejudice of mind, one of Bacon's *idols*, manifesting a desire to see facts in the order in which his personal moral consciousness would like them to have been, is often patent and naïvely manifest; as when, for instance, he says, in a passage on Venetian history in *Stones of Venice :* " I sincerely trust that the inquirer would be disappointed who should endeavor to trace any more immediate reasons for their adoption of the cause of Alexander III. against Barbarossa than the piety which was excited by the character of their suppliant, and the noble pride which provoked the insolence of the Emperor."

When a historical age, or an old master, or one of their works, or one side and feature of the age, master, and work, correspond to the leading feature of Ruskin's moral nature, then his sympathy grows deep and searching, and he is enabled to discover hidden beauties

that were not evident before, and to shed
a brilliant and glowing light over that
which was wrapped in cold gloom. In
other words, Ruskin must admire in order
to be just in his treatment. His mind is
thus diametrically opposed to the ideally
scientific mind summarized epigrammati-
cally by Spinoza in the words, *neque flere,
neque ridere, neque admirari, neque con-
temnere — sed intelligere* — "neither to
weep nor to laugh, neither to admire nor
to despise, but to understand." And I
cannot help believing that Ruskin's treatment of history, more especially of the
history of art, as far as it has had influence, has retarded the progress of the
really scientific investigation of the past,
which in other countries, especially in
Germany, has been fully established and
developed, and has produced such rich
harvest. Great as has been the share
which England has had in the establishment of scientific method in the natural
sciences, the historical sciences, with some
notable exceptions of individual efforts,
have traditionally been retarded in their
growth by the intermixture of interests,

literary, political, or ethical, foreign to and
destructive of the supreme end, namely,
the acquisition of methodical knowledge.
With regard to the study of the history
of art, the result has been that those who
have been inspired by Ruskin have thus
spurned sober historical inquiry and scientific observation, while the really scientific
inquirers in other departments of knowledge have not credited the subject with
the capability of sober methodical treatment, and so, for instance, the introduction of these studies into the recognized
homes of inquiry — the universities — as
topics of serious thought has been de-
layed.

Though, as we shall see, Ruskin in the
main drift of his treatment of nature is
not romantic, in his treatment of man
and his works in the present and in the
past he distinctly is. I think it important for the understanding of what fol-
lows that this term "romantic," used so
loosely and frequently, should be more
clearly defined.

The romantic spirit has ever arisen in
times when people were discontented with

the then existing state of affairs. It primarily manifests itself in its negative character, in the spurning of what is living
and present, and in the attempt at blinding the eye to what is actual, and in so
far ungainly. There is therefore always
a touch of unreality about the romantic.
This negative repulsion from the actual
and present also gives essential color to
its positive features, namely, in making
whatever comes within its pale essentially
different from what is habitually present
in the living. The romanticist thus looks
upon the past because it is past and not
present, and upon the works of fancy because they are fanciful and not real; but
both must have the power of carrying
him away from the oppressive reality to
that which is different from it.

Another essential attribute of the romantic spirit is the desiring attitude of
mind. Though the romanticist looks for
the past because it is past, and upon the
fanciful because it is not real, he does not
look upon them dispassionately, but longingly, with the futile desire, of which he
is half conscious, to make them present

and actual. And while, on the one hand, disporting himself in Rousseauesque nudity, or wrapping himself closely in the sable cloak of Werther, he weakens the vitality of the present and actual by means of his morbidly powerful imagination, on the other hand, his desires have not diminished the remoteness of the past and of the realms of fantasy. Having shed over both the particular light natural to him personally in his fervent longings, and having destroyed his clearness of sight with regard to the present, and disturbed its just proportion, he has not gained in the power of penetrating into the past, which he has also robbed of its true consistency in emasculating his energy of dispassionate retrospection.

The romantic must not be confounded with the historical. I believe that it is not very long that we have emerged out of the romantic period, and that one of the main intellectual features of the age of which ours is the beginning will be the historical habit of mind. It has often been said that the age in which we live is primarily scientific, chiefly marked by the

habit of mind produced and encouraged
by careful observation of the living things
that surround us, **and** by inductive reasoning. Though this be true, it appears
to me none the less **true** that **our** age is
intellectually also marked **by** the **con-**
sideration of the past, and is historical
as much as it is scientific and humanitarian. We also look to the past, perhaps more than any preceding age, yet
distinctly **not** in **the** romantic spirit.
There is no desire mixed up with this in-
terest in the past, no attempt at fleeing
to it, away from the present; for we have
made the past ever present, a real and
actual part of our mental possessions, in
which we can take purely intellectual or
emotionally sympathetic delight as much
as in the living realities before us. More
and more the feeling is spreading among
all people that the knowledge of the past
is a common heritage, and it is becoming
an essential part of the consciousness of
all thinking people, without which no
mind will be considered completely developed and educated. To instance poetry, the nearest field **where** romanticism

has disported itself, it appears to me that Robert Browning in his treatment of the past strongly marks the turning-point of this new historical attitude. To him the past with its life is a great mine, from which treasures may be brought to the surface of the present, adding to the intellectual and artistic wealth of our own days without diminishing the working capital of our moral and useful mental industry. And because he thus breaks through the gates of the past, unburdened by the melancholy weight of morbid desires, he can really penetrate to the depths, whence he returns with genuine jewels, and not with the potsherds and bits of glass and paste that lie this side the gate in the vague unreality of the misty land of romanticism. The less we are romantic, the less we are thus fearful of or opposed to the present, the more likely are we to do justice to history.

Now it appears to me that Ruskin is still strongly enslaved by romanticism, as well in his want of real sympathy with the present, with that which actually is, as in his incapacity to throw off his per-

sonal predilections when dealing with
past ages or with ancient works of art.
So, for instance, he seems to me incapable of appreciating, and wilfully closes his
eyes to, the spirit of ancient Hellas. The
moral and intellectual life of the Greeks
does not appear to him to furnish that
which he personally desires to find, and
therefore he has not been able justly to
appreciate their history nor to feel their
art. And when, as in the *Queen of the
Air*, he does deal with one of their religious works, he transforms, and I must
say often caricatures, it into a lay-figure
hung all over with mystical tinsel. The
healthy brightness and cheerfulness of
this artistic race have not increased his
rich treasure-house with any of its re-
splendent jewels. Nay, it appears to me
that it is partly owing to this want of historical sympathy that, in architecture, his
powerful yet exclusive praise of the Goth-
ic should at the same time have driven
him to the abuse of the Hellenic elements
in Renaissance building. The same feeling has led him to draw such arbitrarily
hard and fast lines between what he con-

siders periods of high development and periods of absolute decline in the life and arts of political communities, as it has also in part been effective in blinding him to the great beauties in the art of whole nations, such as the Dutch. It has led him, and with him many others, because they see the undoubted beauty in child-like simplicity (which the others can appreciate as well as the romanticist), to exaggerate and to hold up for odious comparison, distorting truthful relation, the merits of the early struggling efforts of incomplete art—incomplete not only in execution, but often (but for the suggestion of simplicity contained in the effort, and not in the work itself) even in loftiness of true artistic conception. And it is the romantic projection of his personal religious prejudice which makes him consider imperfection as such, which undoubtedly prevails in all things terrestrial, an artistic virtue, as he does in § 25, chap. vi., Vol. II., in *Stones of Venice*. We meet with much misguided judgment and superficial cant nowadays with regard to the qualities of more *savage* art, and the beauty in the imperfections of technique, and this turbid wave of taste has had a deleterious effect upon art production and manufacture. There may be some rude quality in the early stages of more " savage art," and we may admire these qualities, but in *so far as they are "savage,"* we must never forget they are imperfect. The early or archaic ·periods of art are full of interest and a certain kind of beauty; but considered from the highest artistic point of view they are certainly inferior to the most developed forms. However capable, for instance, we may be to appreciate the qualities of the work of an early Greek sculptor, such as Onatas, the highest spiritual expression of this current of human effort is still to be found in the works of Phidias, towards which the earlier endeavors tend. This is the case in the works of all branches and periods of art. And the fashion which has existed, and is still current, of paradoxically magnifying the merit of the quaint forms of less perfect art, at the cost of the works belonging to the advanced stages, is either due to insincere cant or a mistake in assigning the proper place and proportion to some individual virtue or cause of preference. Still more common appears to be the favor which imperfections of technique find. If certain pieces of Venetian glass-work are undoubtedly superior to the machine-work of the present day, it is not due to the " imperfection " of the work of the hand, nor to the obtrusion of man's labor in executing it, but because the lines are less hard, and the work of man really appears to produce finer linear effects and more beautiful refractions of light. But to reproduce actual faults of structure, which the benighted workers in past ages would gladly have improved upon if they had had the implements and known the processes, to vitiate the healthy life of architecture in new buildings by the wanton reproduction of pathological accidents of time in ancient edifices, constantly to dilute the " architectural " by a superficial infusion of the " pictorial "—as is so frequently done now—is a morbid state of taste in support of which the misguided public and artists can find many a passage

in the writings of Ruskin. In dealing
with the history of art, with the works of
nations and periods and individuals, the
golden rule for the general treatment of
Ruskin's works applies more powerfully
than ever—follow him when he admires,
and fly from him when he disapproves.

II

RUSKIN AS THE FOUNDER OF *PHÆNOM-
ENOLOGY OF NATURE

THE term romantic is also applied to
nature, and here it has fundamentally the
same meaning as when applied to history.
The romantic attitude of mind with regard to nature is again distinguished by
the shunning of the reality that immediately surrounds man ; and though in
the case of nature it is not possible, as it

---

* I have had much hesitation in choosing this term,
which, no doubt, has a pedantic sound. The first word
which suggested itself was " Morphology," which would
have accentuated the study of form as such. But this
term has been seized by modern biologists, and would
thus have been ambiguous. The word '' Phænomenology," I am aware, was in use by mediæval schoolmen.
But the remoteness and obscurity of scholastic writings
made me hesitate less to adopt it in the new and modern
acceptation I have ventured to give it, especially as the
scholastic antithesis between Phænomena and Noou-
mena helps to mark the essential meaning of the term
Phænomenology as here used.

5

is in the case of history and of the world
of imagination, to modify or distort what
bears its testimony in itself and is present
to the senses, still this negative tendency
of romanticism manifests itself in the *selection* which is made among the scenes
of nature. And this romantic scenery is
selected because it has something out of
the common, something that differs from
the actual surroundings of man in his
daily life, and in so far leads him away
from the reality which he dislikes or fails
to appreciate. The gentle rolling pasture,
the stretches beyond the trim flower-garden, reverberating with the busy life of
the village close at hand, are not romantic, excepting, perhaps, by relative gradation, to the dweller in the metropolis;
they are too familiar and actually living.
But the distant lonely crag and ravine,
with the uncommonness of their jagged
outline, set in a scene of desolation, without any suggestion of present human life,
are, apart from the quality of sublimity
which they may possess, and the undoubted specific charm of novelty which unfamiliarity adds to their intrinsic form, more

likely to be considered romantic. This is because of their antithesis to the scenes that are associated with familiar life, and their admixture of unreality, owing to their unfamiliarity, and the absence of associations which tie the imagination of the present-weary romanticist in his flight away from what is before him.

There is, furthermore, the element of desire in the attitude of mind when the romanticist endeavors to appreciate nature. It here manifests itself in that he must needs project himself—that is, man—into the nature that he thus admires. As he did not give an unprejudiced ear to the voice of the past, so he does not permit nature to give the fulness of her story in her own language. There is a predominance of human associations, be it with regard to man's fate in the present or in the past, in this view of nature; and the romanticist is not able to receive completely and unalloyed all the impressions of form and color and concentrated life which give a distinct spiritual organization to natural scenery undisturbed by alien considerations.

Both these elements in the romanticist's
selection of natural scenery have added to
them the further factor that he admixes
with his appreciation of nature those associations **from the** sphere of human **interest that** we have before defined **as** romantic; that he prefers those scenes and effects
of nature which, in so far as they **do sug-**
gest human associations, recall those **that**
are not of the present, but belong **to the**
desired and preferred section of the past.
Then it is not **the rock** jutting over the
sea that is admired in itself, but this only
claims his attention **as a firm** foundation
for the ruined castle in which proud and
chivalrous knights and fair ladies dwelt ;
not the field, with its waving **ears of corn**
and its hedge-rows with all **the delicate**
colors and the world of graceful **lines of**
the growth within **it,** belted by wood and
dale, **but the** field upon which Round-
heads and Cavaliers fought for the Parlia-
ment or King Charles ; spring-tide is not
dressed in its potent and rich transforma-
tion for its own inner beauty, but it is the
season of love ; autumn is **at** most likened
to man's incipient decay ; **clouds** only har-

bor under their swelling robes the shafts of lightning that bode destruction ; and the atmosphere is bright, is clear or dismal, as it best suits the lonely horseman muffled in his cloak.

But in Ruskin we have indeed a revelation of nature in a new light ; and this attitude of mind is distinctly modern, and in its main development has been chiefly English. Perhaps, as running parallel with Wordsworth, the American poets Bryant, Longfellow, Whittier, Emerson, Lowell, and, above all, Thoreau and Burroughs, with their intercourse with nature, and their love for and intimacy with the wealth of beautiful trees in which the New England and Middle States abound, may be quoted. But they, as well as Keats, Southey, and Tennyson, do not form the distinct landmarks which the four names here following indicate. The Greeks, though they were in nowise romantic—in fact were distinctly opposed to that frame of mind—were so thoroughly and pronouncedly human in their whole mental organization that they did not develop this form of appreciation. They

constantly projected man—though actual, present man—into nature, and endowed **her with** life like their own, so vivid that they could always hold friendly communion with **her.** Further, she harbored the life of **their** gods, and their **gods were thus** familiarly present to them. **But to** study and admire her for her **own inner** beauty of form and color, as they studied and admired the human form for its own pure sake, was a stage of æsthetic development to which they did not attain. And in **the** whole range of literature, down to our **own** days, so far as I am acquainted with **it** and **as** I have **been able to recall its** treatment of nature, there is no manifestation of the habitual and sustained effort of describing and dealing with nature **for** her own sake, independent **of human associations.** **Spring and** summer, valleys and mountains, meadows and flowers, rain and sunshine, are indeed dealt with ; but **in** the dealing with them there is no manifestation of real observation of their form, nor is there a pure and concentrated interest **in** them for their own **sake.** If they are not themselves anthropomorphic, his-

torical, **or romantic,** they are at most bu-
colic **or** idyllic in their treatment.

The beginnings of this new epoch are
quite recent, and they are, as I believe, **to**
be found in a writer who in his main features is considered the arch - romanticist,
namely, Byron, **in** one **of** his works,
"Childe Harold." Of course in this poem
we have much description of scenery
which would be classed under the head
of romantic, and I only mean that in him
we have the beginnings of a designed and
concentrated desire of dwelling upon the
scenes, making their own inner harmony
the chief point of artistic interest. The
next stage **in** this development I find in
Shelley; and though in him the warmth
of his humanitarian interest, **which gives**
its stamp to his lyrical genius, always
makes its strength felt, especially **in the**
human imagery he uses in describing nat-
ure, still we feel the genuine touch of the
true sympathetic observer, whether it be
in the awful stillness of the mountain
heights, or in the rush of the west wind
driving the withered leaves, or even in the
fantastic description of Alastor's mount-

ain chasm. And the next marked step is
made by Wordsworth, who trains the eye
to watch and perceive even the petals of
simple little flowers; though in him, again,
there is a preponderance of the didactic
habit. But the highest stage yet reached
in this direction, a new departure, in fact,
in the character of man's observation, is
made by Ruskin. These four men appear
to me to mark the advance. The claims
of many have been considered, and have
been rejected as either not falling under
this head at all, or not marking distinct
steps in this progression. I have carefully considered, for instance, the claims of
Scott; but I have felt that his descriptions
are either romantic, or, at least, that they
are always marked by a subordination to
some main human interest or event in
the poem or story. And it is especially
curious to note that there is great difficulty in including among their number any
of the German, French, or Italian poets.
And though Goethe is less romantic in
his description than Schiller or Uhland,
his descriptive lyrics are more directly
expressions of moods evoked by, or cast-

ing their light over, the objects described; while **Lamartine and** Victor Hugo strike **me as** romantic, idyllic, or didactic. The chief developers of this habit of mind are thus all English; and when the important position which England has held **in the** development of the **art** of landscape-painting **in** its highest form **is** taken **into** account, I may venture **to** give my individual experience in **a** case where **it is** difficult to collect data to a degree sufficient to warrant **the** formulating **of a** generalization with any pretense to scientific weight of evidence. Having directed my attention to the question, I have found in my travels that, whereas **the** non-English travellers I met would only comment upon more striking and uncommon scenes, and would generally be seeking for and dwelling upon historical associations or features of human or poetical or scientific interest, the English travellers corresponding **to** them would manifest a more penetrating **interest in all** classes **of** scenery, and **a** more habitual power **of** observing, and thus **of** appreciating, forms themselves. They seem to have in **their**

memory a store of lines and colors and
trees and plants and cloud forms and days
of various qualities of light which enable
them to differentiate more intelligently
what is before their eyes. This may be
due to the fact that the more educated
classes of Englishmen have in great numbers been bred and have lived in the country, where the occupation in the garden
and especially the familiar frequent accomplishment of water-color drawing,
where the walks of the women and the
field-sports of the men, have encouraged
such observation. Furthermore, the fact
that the English are a travelling nation
must have contributed to this power; and
finally, perhaps, also the importance which
atmospheric changes have in a country
where they are as frequent as they are expected, and are of importance to the leisure occupations of the dwellers in the
country, may have directed their attention to these facts, and led to the formation of a habit and to the growth of a
faculty which could be utilized in a purely artistic spirit without any further interest of personal comfort or use.

As the true landscape-painter has given us pleasure in the new harmonious soul he has infused into the nature he presents by his truthfully executed composition, and has added a new genus of pictorial art to sacred, mythical, historical, genre, and portrait painting, so Ruskin has insisted upon and developed a new form and habit of observation of nature which can make of us landscape-painters for the nonce, gaining all the delight which is inherent in great pictures themselves, without any of the painful effort necessary for the execution of these works by the brush or the pencil. He has thereby increased our capital of ennobling pleasures, opening out to us fields of delight in the things that are before us, without diminishing their inherent virtue or utility, and without thereby infringing upon the possible good which our neighbors may derive from them. I feel confident that whoever has read the works of Ruskin will thereafter approach nature with a new faculty of appreciation, will have his attention directed to what he before passed by with indifference, and will discover

what before was hidden; and that even
those who possessed this habit of mind
before will have it intensified and enlarged
by the guidance which he will have given
them. And this will not be only with regard to the beauties of the Alps or the
stormy sea, but they will be able to ex-
tract elevating pleasure out of each flower
that blooms before their window in the
summer, and even out of the graceful
tracery-work of the bare branches of the
tree, deadened by the cold winter, that
stands in dreary loneliness at the back of
their town house or in the city square.
And whether it be bright or misty, whether it mean sunshine or rain, each cloud
will become to them a fountain of unselfish joy, having before merely been the
source of anxiety or anticipation.

"It is a strange thing," he says, "how little
in general people know about the sky ; it is the
part of creation in which nature has done more
for the sake of pleasing man, more for the sole
and evident purpose of talking to him and
teaching him, than any other of her works, and
it is just the part in which we least attend to
her. There are not many of her other works

in which some more material or essential purpose than the mere pleasing of man is not answered by every part of their organization ; but
every essential purpose of the sky might, so far
as we know, be answered, if once in three days
or thereabouts a great, ugly, black, round cloud
were brought up over the blue, and everything
well watered, and was left blue again till next
time, with perhaps a film of morning and even-
ing mist for dew. And instead of this there is
not a moment of any day of our lives when
nature is not producing scene after scene, picture after picture, glory after glory, and working still upon such exquisite and constant principles of the most perfect beauty that it is quite
certain it is all done for us and intended for
our perpetual pleasure. And every man, wherever placed, however far from the other sources
of interest or beauty, has this doing for him
constantly. The noblest scenes of the earth
can be seen and known but by few; it is not
intended that man should live always in the
midst of them, he injures them by his presence;
he ceases to feel them if he be always with
them ; but the sky is for all ; bright as it is, it
is not 'too bright, nor good, for human nature's daily food ;' it is fitted in all its functions
for the perpetual comfort and exalting of the
heart, for the soothing it and purifying it from

its **dross** and dust. Sometimes gentle, sometimes capricious, sometimes awful, never the
same for two moments together ; almost human
in its passions, almost spiritual in its tender-
ness, almost **divine in its** infinity, **its** appeal to
what is immortal in **us is as** distinct as its min-
istry of chastisement or of blessing **to what is**
mortal or essential. And yet we never **attend**
to it, **we never** make it a subject of thought,
but as it has to do with our animal sensations ;
we look upon all by which it speaks to us more
clearly than to brutes, upon all which bears wit-
ness to the intention **of** the Supreme, that we
are to receive more from the covering vault
than the light and the dew which we share
with the weed and the worm, only **as a** succes-
sion of meaningless and monotonous accidents,
too common and too vain to be worthy **of a**
moment of watchfulness or a glance **of admira-**
tion   If in our moments of **utter idleness or**
insipidity we turn to the sky as a **last resource,**
which of its phenomena do we speak **of ?**   One
says it has been wet, and another it has **been**
windy, and another it has been **warm.**   Who
among the whole chattering crowd can tell one
of the forms and precipices **of** the chain of tall
white mountains **that** girded the horizon at
noon **yesterday ?** Who saw **the** narrow **sun-**
beam **that came out** of the south and smote

upon their summits until they melted and mouldered away in a dust of blue rain? Who saw the dance of the dead clouds when the sunlight left them last night, and the west wind blew them before it like withered leaves? All has passed unregretted as unseen ; or if the apathy be ever shaken off, even for an instant, it is only by what is gross or what is extraordinary ; and yet it is not in the broad and fierce manifestations of the elemental energies, not in the clash of the hail nor the drift of the whirlwind, that the highest characters of the sublime are developed. God is not in the earthquake nor in the fire, but in the still small voice. They are but the blunt and the low faculties of our nature which can only be addressed through lampblack and lightning. It is in quiet and subdued passages of unobtrusive majesty, the dry and the calm and the perpetual—that which must be sought ere it is seen, and loved ere it is understood—things which the angels work out for us daily and yet very eternally, which are never wanting and never repeated, which are to be found always, yet each found but once ; it is through these that the lesson is chiefly taught, and the blessing of beauty given. These are what the artist of highest aim must study ; it is these by the combination of which his ideal is to be created ;

these, of which so little notice is ordinarily taken by common observers that I fully believe, little as people in general are concerned with art, more of their ideas of sky are derived from pictures than from reality, and that if we could examine the conception formed in the minds of most educated persons when we talk of clouds, it would frequently be found composed of fragments of blue and white reminiscences of the old masters."—*Modern Painters*, vol. i., sec. iii., chap. i.

Thus it is, despite the didactic strain introduced here and elsewhere, that Ruskin can make non-painting painters of every man and woman. In our leisure walks, as well as in proceeding from one task to another through fields, and, for that, even through streets (and he and others with him would devoutly wish that the hand of man would give more opportunity for this pleasure in the streets of towns), we can create for ourselves these pictures within our own minds. It is true, its direct purpose is merely to give him personal pleasure. Although, beyond this, he may transmit this habit to those about him, and be a unit of what may be formed into a national characteristic; still it does not diminish the pleasure-giving capacity or use of what has thus caused him delight, nor does he thereby interfere with the pleasure and activity of his neighbor.

All this concerns the purely artistic attitude of mind with regard to nature. But original and fundamental as may have been Ruskin's work in this direction, it is still more so in the further outcome of this line of thought, in which, it appears to me, he has made the beginning for a quite new sphere of mental discipline—a sphere that lies, as I have before said, on the border line between art and science, overlapping into both. For want of a better term, I should call this Phæ-nomenology of Nature. The main drift and character of this species of observation is perhaps artistic; yet it is also markedly cognitive and wittingly systematic, and thus within the range of science. It differs from science not only in that it has the essential attribute of producing æsthetic pleasure, but especially in that it is concerned, above all things, with

6

the actual appearance and form of what presents itself to man's perceptive faculties as he uses them in ordinary life. He then perceives, unaided by the mechanical devices which are to strengthen his senses beyond their ordinary capacity, such as the microscope and telescope (and, for that, even instantaneous photography), and in not making his perception ancillary and subservient to the primarily scientific aims of discovering laws and controlling causality. It is thus not Nooumenology, but Phænomenology, and if it should advance to the establishment and recognition of "laws," these laws, or rather the generalization from individual experiences and the recognition of constancy within multiplicity and variety, will always be essentially concerned with the form and appearance as such, and not in any way primarily with the process of origin, growth, and development. Ruskin, as far as his work in this sphere is concerned, would consider the nature of the configuration of the earth's surface, the relation between the valley and the mountain and the plain and the shore, endeavor-

ing to discover what is constant within its
manifoldness, considering only its form
and appearance as such, not as the geologist, whose chief attention must be directed towards the apprehension of the
causes which underlie changes. And
wherever Ruskin has unwittingly desert-
ed this chief vocation, to which his genius
has called him for the world's good, and
has confused the clearness of his original
attitude of mind by the feeble intrusion
of that of the geologist and the man of
science in general, he has tarnished the
pure metal of his work, has desecrated the
shrine of true science, and has created an
artificial antithesis between his own view
of things and that of the professed and
conscientious scientist, which has lowered
the sphere of each in the eyes of the followers of either. So also Ruskin can examine the form and color of rocks and
stones, and can dwell upon their constancy, without in the least being a min-
eralogist, nor deserving censure when
judged as such, in spite of what he has
done to deserve it ; and so with regard to
plants, animals, and man, without being a

scientific botanist or biologist or an anthropologist.

And as regards the sky, he turns his and our observation to its phenomena, not as the physicist nor as the meteorologist would do, not to prognosticate fine or fair weather, or to record the causes of its changes, nor to rob the universe of the secret of its unseen fundamental laws of motion, not to deal with atoms and molecules; but to discover, if such there be, the laws of harmony and of continuousness in the changes of its form as such, and carefully to use in all this, if it be fitting to do so, the knowledge which science gives from its own deeply moral point of view.

I am not justified, from lack of sufficient observation on my own part, to estimate critically the exact degree in which in every instance Ruskin's observations in this respect are thorough and careful; and from the general tenor of much of his reasoning in other spheres, I cannot help fearing that he may at times have been carried away in his recording of general phenomena, for the perception of

which he undoubtedly has such exceptionally favorable predisposition. But
be this as it may, so much is clear to me,
that he has pointed out to the observer
a fertile field of inquiry of a new order
and a new department of knowledge ; and
there is no reason why, in the future,
those whose pursuits lie absolutely in the
spheres of science, yet who thus have exceptional material opportunities for observation, such as geologists, biologists, and
still more the workers of our meteoro-
logical stations, should not take up and
follow out this class of observation in the
main spirit of Ruskin. Take, for instance,
his division of the clouds into their three
regions of the sky, the upper region of
the cirrus, the central region of the stratus,
the lower region of the rain cloud, and
his classification of their distinctive forms
and colors, and their movement and
change, as he beautifully describes them
in section iii. of the first volume of *Modern
Painters*, which will fully exemplify what
I here mean. His work in this department alone will secure for him a position
in the company of the world's great ben-

efactors which will have vitality to out-
live and outlast all the shortcomings
which block his way to the gates of unre-
served approbation and acceptance; and
the sooner **we** can dissipate the dross of
his failings from the gold of his virtues,
the sooner will the world realize its **own**
gain. And it is thus even in this sphere
of his greatest work that I must again
point to a limitation, again consisting in
the inopportune introduction of his religious and didactic bias, which darkens
the lucidity of his observation, and often
counteracts the good effects his teaching
would **otherwise have.** I have before
pointed to the good which every reader
of Ruskin must derive from **his works, in**
having his eyes turned towards **a fuller**
appreciation **of** nature. But **I cannot**
help feeling **the** danger **which his** rapid
and lawless incursions **into** the **province**
of science may have in encouraging that
great vice of the general public, namely,
dilettanteism in the study of the Phænomenology of Nature. I cannot help feeling
also that much good as may be done to
children **in** producing **in** them **the love**

and faculty of observation, and in reading to them selected passages from his works (among which I should carefully avoid all those that have the morbidly didactic tone in his books for children and girls), one must guard against the danger of blunting their faculty for and reverence of accurate truthfulness, in mixing up fancy with systematic truth, as is done, for instance, with regard to flowers in his *Proserpina.* An undisguised fairy tale on the one hand, and a botanical primer, or, still better, an intelligent and sympathetic companion in the garden and in country walks, on the other, would avoid the danger I apprehend. But with these reservations, which I have thought it right to make, this portion of his work remains of the greatest value, and its value is increased by the opportunities it has afforded him for the production of those works of literary power seen at its fullest height in his treatment of nature as a writer and prose poet.

III

RUSKIN AS A WRITER AND PROSE POET

IT may be felt by superficial readers of his works that his power of diction and unsurpassed command over words and their musical quality has been used at the expense of his power of describing with accuracy. Yet it is one of the most astonishing and admirable qualities of his best passages that, with all their alliteration and the harmony of sound which pervades his ordered array, the description is most minute and accurate; and no better words, no words encircling and penetrating the meaning of things more fully and promptly, could have been chosen. We are inclined to approach such passages with the primary doubt that they are too good to be true, that they are too fine in form, too much adorned and bedecked, to serve the hard every-day use of adequate transmission of meaning. Yet if we compare any one thing we know familiarly with Ruskin's description of it, if we attempt before-hand to transcribe it into sober accurate words, devoid of form and rhythm, and then compare our own description with that of Ruskin, from the point of view of their respective adequacy of transmission of meaning, we shall find that Ruskin's description, in addition to the beauty of form, contains also a more exhaustive enumeration of attributes, and a better selection of the features that give dis-tinctive essence to the thing described. In the range of all his writings I can hardly think of a more illustrative pas-sage than one, published quite recently in his *Præterita*, describing the Rhone :

"For all other rivers there is a surface, and an underneath, and a vaguely displeasing idea of the bottom. But the Rhone flows like one lambent jewel ; its surface is nowhere, its ethe-real self is everywhere, the iridescent rush and translucent strength of it, blue to the shore and radiant to the depth.

"Fifteen feet thick, of not flowing but fly-

ing water ; not water, neither—melted glacier,
rather, one should call it. The **force** of the ice
is with it, and the wreathing of **the clouds, the**
gladness **of the sky, and the** continuance **of**
Time.

" Waves of clear **sea are, indeed, lovely to**
watch, but they are **always coming or gone,**
never in **a** taken shape to **be seen for a second.**
But here was one mighty wave that was **always**
itself, and every fluted swirl of **it constant as**
the wreathing of a shell. No wasting away **of**
the fallen foam, no pause for gathering of pow-
er, no hopeless ebb of discouraged recoil ; **but**
alike through bright day and lulling night, the
never-pausing plunge, **and** never-fading flash,
and never-hushing whisper, and while the sun
was up, the ever-answering glow of unearthly
aquamarine, ultramarine, violet blue, **gentian**
blue, peacock blue, river-of-paradise blue, **glass**
of a painted window melted in **the sun, and the**
witch **of** the Alps flinging **the spun tresses of it**
forever from her snow.

" The innocent way, too, in which the river
used to stop to look into every little corner.
Great **torrents** always seem angry, and great
rivers too often sullen ; **but** there is no anger,
no disdain, in the **Rhone.** It seemed as if the
mountain stream was in mere bliss **at recover-**
ing itself again out of the lake sleep, and raced

because it rejoiced in racing, fain yet to return and **stay.** There were pieces of wave that danced all day as if Perdita were looking on to learn ; there were little streams that skipped like lambs and leaped like chamois ; there were pools that shook the sunshine all through them, and were rippled **in layers of** overlaid ripples, like **crystal sand; there** were **currents that** twisted **the light into golden braids, and inlaid** the **threads with turquoise enamel ; there were** strips **of stream that had certainly above the** lake been mill-streams, **and** were looking busi-**ly for** mills to turn again ; there were shoots **of stream** that had once shot fearfully into the **air, and now** sprang up again laughing that **they** had only fallen **a** foot or two : and in the midst of all the gay glittering and eddied lingering, the noble bearing by of **the midmost** depth, so mighty, yet so terrorless and harmless, with its swallows skimming instead of petrels, and the dear old decrepit town as safe in the embracing sweep of it as if it were set in a brooch of sapphire."

Critics **of** the stereotyped order may doubt whether such lyrical prose **is** at all justifiable, or whether alliteration is not a blemish in **prose** writing. They may measure with their joiner's rod and weigh in their chemist's scale; but the fact remains that so far as written words have a justification, their sound and sequence have or ought to have a function in conveying adequately the meaning, as much as their immediate grammatical symbolism.

Lessing, in his fundamental, though somewhat narrow, work on criticism, *Laokoon*, in which he defines the province of the various arts, especially painting and poetry, has drawn attention to the chief distinctive means of expression of the various arts, which necessarily define and modify their different provinces. Painting and sculpture find expression by means of material form and color, literature and poetry by means of words. The pictorial and plastic arts are the arts of space-continuity, and thus differ essentially from the literary arts, which deal with time-succession, in which words are read and heard. Whereas the chief characteristic of pictorial art in its description is the harmony of things as they actually coexist at any given time, the chief element of description in words is succession, and this succession can only inadequately reproduce the complete impression of actual coexistence. Lessing thus maintains that, in conformity with this essential nature of word description, the best and most successful endeavors must correspond to it; and whereas sculpture and painting are not most adapted to the rendering of movement and action, and can only attain this by the most expressive and life - suggesting moments of repose, poetic description is not best adapted, on its side, to the conveyance of images the essence of which is the complete unity of their parts in the repose of each moment. When poetry does attempt to describe things in repose, it does it best by means of the manifestation of the unity of the body or scene, and the interrelation of their parts in movement and action. He is no doubt right when he considers the dramatic form of description most naturally adapted to literature; but he appears to me to overshoot the mark in too emphatically excluding the enumeration of the individual features of the object de-

scribed, which can be done in a really literary and poetic manner. We must not
forget that the habit of looking **upon**
paintings has, **in the** course of ages, given
a pictorial faculty to our mind **as a whole,**
and that modern man, without an effort,
can reconstruct into a new picture of the
inner eye the detached portions of the image which are transmitted to him through
the ear, provided there is added another
sensuous vehicle, tending towards this so-
lidification, and directly producing unity
in his general mood, in the color of which
the disjointed sound-units will naturally
be united. This accompanying sensuous
element I should characterize in one
word as the lyrical factor, **whether in**
poetry or prose. **It is** this element **which**
supplies **the** requisite insisted **upon by**
Lessing in his "dramatic character **of**
word description" when he points out
that we are, for instance, more likely to
receive an adequate impression of the appearance of a man if, as poetry can best
do, the impression which his person and
his actions make upon others is given,
rather than the enumeration **of his indi-**

vidual features, such as the color of his
eyes, the shape of his nose, and the pro-
portions of his figure. In this dramatic
form of description the element of sympathy is called into play, which produces
definite moods in us, and sensualizes and
solidifies the vague units of sounds in time
and succession into the actual consistency
of an image. Now I hold that with regard to scenes in nature in especial this
sympathetic chord of inner mood (*Stim-
mung*) is supplied by that element of
sound in which the quality of the word
and the expressive harmony of the con-
text, together with general rhythm and
structure directly, sensuously (like a musical accompaniment), create a sympathetic mood, which lasts through the succession of time in which the description
is read or heard, and gives its bodily unity and tangibility to each word-unit that
would otherwise die the moment its actual
sound is ended. I think that one of the
model instances of the poetic power in
description of nature with all these elements combined is contained in the short
yet powerful description of Moldavian

scenery in the opening of Browning's "Flight of the Duchess." Ruskin in his best descriptions of nature does also use movement as the central energy of his descriptive motive. Clouds are not merely square or round or multiform, but they move, swing, sweep, or hang to and in their various shapes; their colors are growing or fading in intensity, or asserting some relation to one another; nay, even the shape of each rock and stone and leaf and twig is described in the varied motion of its lines. He also appeals to dramatic sympathy in recalling the analogies of human or animal life. But above all, he has succeeded in breaking into Lessing's forbidden boundaries of enumeration, because his progressive account is fixed and chained into unity and harmony by this lyrical character of his prose. Take, for instance, his poetic rendering of Turner's *picture* of Babylon, and in this accurate enumeration we feel that there is a justifiable and adequate transliteration of the details of a scene.

"Ten miles away, down the Euphrates,

where it gleams last along the plain, he gives
us a drift of dark elongated vapor, melted beneath into a dim haze which embraces the hills
on the horizon. It is exhausted with its own
motion, and broken by the wind in its own
body into numberless groups of billowy and
tossing fragments, which, beaten by the weight
of storm down to earth, are just lifting themselves again on wearied wings, and perishing
in the effort. Above these, and far beyond
them, the eye goes back to a broad sea of white
illuminated mist, or rather cloud melted into
rain, and absorbed again before that rain has
fallen, but penetrated throughout, whether it
be vapor or whether it be dew, with soft sunshine turning it as white as snow. Gradually,
as it rises, the rainy fusion ceases ; you cannot
tell where the film of blue on the left begins—
but it is deepening, deepening still—and the
cloud, with its edge first invisible, then all but
imaginary, then just felt when the eye is *not*
fixed on it and lost when it is, at last rises keen
from excessive distance, but soft and mantling
in its body as a swan's bosom fretted by faint
wind, heaving fitfully against the delicate deep
blue, with white waves, whose forms are traced
by the pale lines of opalescent shadow, shade
only because the light is within it and not upon
it, and which break with their own swiftness

7

into a driven line of level spray, winnowed into
threads by the wind, and flung before the following vapor like those swift shafts of arrowy
water which a great cataract shoots into the
air beside it, trying to find the earth. Beyond
these, again, rises a colossal mountain of gray
cumulus, through whose shadowed sides the
sunbeams penetrate in dim, sloping, rain-like
shafts, and over which they fall in a broad
burst of streaming light, sinking to the earth,
and showing through their own visible radiance
the three successive ranges of hills which con-
nect its desolate plain with space. Above, the
edgy summit of the cumulus, broken into fragments, recedes into the sky, which is peopled
in its serenity with quiet multitudes of the
white, soft, silent cirrus, and under these again
drift near the zenith disturbed and impatient
shadows of a darker spirit, seeking rest and
finding none."—*Modern Painters*, vol. i., chap.
iii., sec. 16.

No doubt the effectiveness of such a
description depends to a great extent
upon the movement which he puts into
every part of his description ; but besides
that, the whole is transferred from life-
less enumeration to a vivid image before
the eyes of the spectator, because of the

assistance of that lyrical element in which the quality of the words, such as, " drift of dark elongated vapor," " billowy and tossing fragments," " film of blue," " keen from excessive distance," " swan's bosom fretted by faint wind," " broad burst of streaming light," "quiet multitudes of the white, soft, silent cirrus," gives sensuous consistency to the momentary sound - suggestion of a word. Further, the very succession of sounds themselves is used to evoke actual emotional sympathy in the hearer with unemotional nature ; so that when after the rain the rainy fusion melts into blue, and he introduces the parenthetical phrases telling us of its " deepening, deepening still," this repetition causes the reader, by the effort of catching the same sound twice over, to experience an inner process corresponding to the gradual gradation in the tone and color which Turner gives at once in material presence. Furthermore, the general rise and fall and cadence of the rhythm help in the same way to express sensuously what the words themselves could only give in their inadequate

disjointed manner; as when, in the sen-
tence with regard to the background beginning, "Above these and far beyond
them," **the first** two-thirds move upward
in a **stronger** impetus, suggesting **the**
varied restlessness in line **and** color **of**
rain clouds, the movement is, as **it were,**
turned downward again towards **repose,**
and conciliated in the rhythm of **the end-**
ing parts **of** the period beginning, "**but**
penetrated throughout;" and this downward movement **or** lower notes that com-
plete the whole **of this** description har-
monize with the final image of the "**dark-**
er spirit seeking rest and finding none."
If one were further to analyze passages
like this, one would find that in the structure of the whole, in the rise **and fall of**
rhythm, and the composition **of these con-**
tinuous waves of sound, they correspond
to and enforce **the** definite meaning and
import of the thoughts and scenes con-
veyed.

Yet, in my opinion, **in** no passage has
he succeeded so completely in giving **ar-**
tistic organization and life to the phenomena of nature **as** such, **as in his descrip-**

tion of the sky's history during one day, viewed from the Alps.

"Stand upon the peak of some isolated mountain at daybreak, when the night mists first rise from off the plains, and watch their white and lake-like fields as they float in level bays and winding gulfs about the islanded summits of the lower hills, untouched yet by more than dawn, colder and more quiet than a windless sea under the moon of midnight; watch when the first sunbeam is sent upon the silver channels, how the foam of their undulating surface parts and passes away; and down under their depths the glittering city and green pasture lie like Atlantis between the white paths of winding rivers, the flakes of light falling every moment faster and broader among the starry spires as the wreathed surges break and vanish above them, and the confused crests and ridges of the dark hills shorten their gray shadows upon the plain. Wait a little longer and you shall see those scattered mists rallying in the ravines, and floating up towards you along the winding valleys, till they couch in quiet masses, iridescent with the morning light, upon the broad breasts of the higher hills, whose leagues of massy undulation will melt back and back into that robe of material light, until they fade

away, lost in its lustre, to appear again **above,**
in the serene heaven, **like a** wild, bright, im-
possible dream, **fou**ndationless and inaccessi-
ble, their very bases **vanishing** in the unsub-
stantial **and** mocking **blue of the** deep lake below. **Wait yet a little** longer **and you** shall see
those **mists** gather themselves into white tow-
ers, and stand like fortresses along the promon-
tories, massy and motionless, only **piled with**
every instant higher and higher **into the sky,**
and casting longer shadows athwart the **rocks;**
and out of the pale blue of the horizon you will
see forming and advancing **a troop** of narrow,
dark, pointed vapors, which will cover the sky,
inch by inch, **with** their gray net-work, and
take the light **off the** landscape with an eclipse
which will stop the singing of the birds and the
motion of the leaves together ; and then you
will see horizontal bars of black shadow forming under them, and **lurid** wreaths **create them-**
selves, you know not how**, along** the shoulders
of the hills ; you never see them form, but when
you look back to a place which was clear an instant ago, there is a cloud on **it,** hanging by the
precipices, as a hawk pauses over his prey. And
then you will hear the sudden rush of the awakened wind, and you will see those watch-tow-
ers of vapor swept away from their foundations,
and waving curtains of opaque rain let **down to**

the valleys, swinging from the burdened clouds
in black bending fringes, or pacing in pale col-
umns along the lake level, grazing its surface
into foam as they go. And then as the sun
sinks you shall see the storm drift for an instant
from off the hills, leaving their broad sides
smoking, and loaded yet with snow-white, torn,
steam-like rays of capricious vapor, now gone,
now gathered again, while the smouldering
sun, seeming not far away, but burning like a
red-hot ball beside you, and as if you could
reach it, plunges through the rushing wind and
rolling cloud with headlong fall, as if it meant
to rise no more, dyeing all the air about it with
blood. And then you shall hear the fainting
tempest die in the hollow of the night, and you
shall see a green halo kindling on the summit
of the eastern hills, brighter, brighter yet, till
the large white circle of the slow moon is lifted
up among the barred clouds, step by step, line
by line; star after star she quenches with her
kindling light, setting in their stead an army
of pale, penetrable, fleecy wreaths in the heav-
en, to give light upon the earth, which move
together, hand in hand, company by company,
troop by troop, so measured in their unity of
motion that the whole heaven seems to roll
with them, and the earth to reel under them.
And then wait yet for one hour, until the east

again becomes purple, and the heaving mountains, rolling against it in darkness like waves
of a wild sea, are drowned one by one in the
glory of its burning ; watch the white glaciers
blaze in their winding paths about the mountains, like mighty serpents with scales of fire ;
watch the columnar peaks of solitary snow,
kindling downward, chasm by chasm, each in
itself a new morning ; their long avalanches
cast down in keen streams brighter than the
lightning, sending each its tribute of driven
snow-like altar smoke up to heaven ; the rose-
light of their silent domes flushing that heaven
about them or above them, piercing with purer
light through its purple lines of lifted cloud,
casting a new glory on every wreath as it passes by, until the whole heaven—one scarlet can-
opy—is interwoven with a roof of waving flame,
and tossing, vault beyond vault, as with the
drifted wings of many companies of angels ;
and then, when you can look no more for gladness, and when you are bowed down with fear
and love of the Maker and Doer of all this, tell
me who has best delivered this His message
unto men !"—*Modern Painters*, vol. i., end of
chap. iv.

Ruskin as a writer of English stands
unrivalled, except perhaps by Shelley, for

the completeness and wealth of his vo-
cabulary (which we must marvel at still
more when we are told by him in his
Præterita that he always wrote easily,
without any struggle), and for his feeling
for the quality of words. It is to be re-
gretted that he sometimes chooses to give
paradoxical significance and restricted de-
notations of his own to ordinary words,
especially in his more sober and theoretical expositions, as when, in chapter iii.
of Vol. i., *Modern Painters*, he calls the
words *mystery* and *inadequacy* elements
of power, or uses the word *particular*
where he means essential; or speaks of
historical truths where he means essential
truths, or defines excellent or pretty or
any other ordinary term in an extraordinary manner. But these irritating confusions, which also apply to the titles of
his books, generally occur in his more
scientific disquisitions, where, it is true,
they do incalculable harm in misleading
him as well as his readers; and I feel certain that the use that he makes of the
word *imperfection* or *particular* and
many others is at the bottom of many

fallacies into which he has been led and leads others. But where he is purely descriptive this does not happen to the same degree.

Within the variety of rhythmical changes which he introduces in harmony with the meaning he conveys, there is one general rhythm peculiarly his own; it has, if I may so say, a gentle undulating character, swelling gradually to a point of general position, and then dying away into what almost appears a minor key in a negative limitation, with which minor key his periods generally end. That there is such a general character to the rhythm of his writings can here be illustrated by comparing in this respect parts of the passage, from which I have quoted, on the open sky with some in the description of the Rhone. Compare, for instance, with regard to their rhythmical arrangement, the passage on the Rhone beginning, " For all other rivers there is a surface," etc., and then its limitation down to " radiant to the depth," with the passage on the sky beginning with " The noblest scenes of the earth," and ending with " purifying

it from its dross and dust." Compare,
again, this last passage, from its beginning
down to "what is mortal or essential,"
with another paragraph in the Rhone description beginning with " Waves of clear
sea are," and ending with "forever from
her snow," and I am sure my meaning
will be clear. This beautiful rise and fall
of cadence is probably due to his early
and constant reading of the Bible, and
especially the rhythmical responsion in
the Psalms; and there is no doubt that
his feeling for words and much of his
grand style originally are derived from
the same source. He is often quite biblical in the character of his diction, especially when he is preaching. Take, for
instance, the passage from paragraph 5
to 8 in the chapter on the Theoretic Faculty in the second volume of *Modern
Painters*, where he inveighs against "the
vine-dressers and husbandmen who love
the corn they grind and the grapes they
crush better than the gardens of the angels
upon the slopes of Eden ; hewers of wood
and drawers of water, who think that the
wood they hew and the water they draw

are better than the pine forests that cover **the** mountains **like** the shadow of God, **and** than the great rivers that move like **His** eternity," etc. **No** doubt he owes much of **the beauty of** his style to his early Bible-reading, and **we feel** its powerful influence especially where he **is** solemn or divinely simple in his description. Even his simplicity is thus biblical and **weighty.** But its influence has not always been for the good; for it has sometimes counter**acted** clearness and sobriety of diction in ordinary language, and in its quasi-archaic character it is not really simple in the modern sense, though **it be** simple in its primitive weightiness. And often, when he means to be sober and analytical, his mood becomes exalted, and is carried **to a** high **pitch,** leading **to a** diction **that is** too strongly lyrical and antithetical, when he **ought** to be merely simple, lucid, and sober. His apparent sobriety is then almost ironical sobriety, and has the appearance of trembling with sustained emotion. This habit is not conducive to the best work when he means **to** be purely theoretical. On the other hand, there are pas-

sages of **powerful** sober **antithesis,** such
as we find in his warning to young art-
ists against brilliancy of execution **or ef-**
forts at invention, in the 20th paragraph
of chapter iii., section 6, Part II., of *Modern Painters;* and here also he manifests
his power **of** epigram, which **the more**
diffuse character **of his** writings would
not lead **us to** expect. But when he does
indulge in aphorisms, they are very good,
as, for instance, his epigrammatic definition of symmetry as contrasted with proportion : " Symmetry is *opposition* of *equal*
quantities to each other, proportion the
connection of *unequal* quantities with each
other." **Or another :** " All copyists are
contemptible, but the copyist **of** himself
is the most so, for he has the **worst** original." The latter epigram also has a touch
of ironical humor, which he often manifests, as when he reviles Gaspar Poussin's
picture of a storm : " Storms, indeed, as
the innocent public insist on calling such
abuses of nature and abortions of art as
the two windy Gaspars **in our** National
Gallery, are common enough — massive
concretions of ink and indigo wrung and

twisted very hard, apparently in a vain effort to get some moisture out of them,
bearing up courageously and successfully
against a wind whose effects on the trees
in the foreground can be accounted for
only on the supposition that they are all
of the India-rubber species." But genuine
light humor is not made to his hand, and
there are more traces of it in his latest
work, *Præterita*, than in any of his previous writings.   For this he has not sufficient sympathy with the real healthy life
that surrounds him ; and in spite of his
noble humanitarian preaching and his still
nobler philanthropic life and example, his
works do not set before us a man of wide
and real sympathies with the life about
him.   The publication of his *Præterita*
shows how deficient his education was in
encouraging this side in him.   This makes
him all the greater ; yet it must have
hampered him frequently in the just consideration of social, economical, and political questions.

IV

RUSKIN AS A WRITER ON SOCIAL, POLITICAL, AND ECONOMICAL QUESTIONS

IN the field of practical ethics and politics Ruskin's tendency to preach finds a more suitable and just scope than in the more theoretical spheres of his literary activity. And his great literary power of diction has enabled him to give new form and emphasis to principles that have almost been adopted by us as moral commonplaces, however little they may have been acted upon, and do show in glaring light the contradiction which obtains between the higher moral and religious tenets and the ordinary working traditions of modern society. He has thus become one of the foremost writers on what might be called practical sociology or economic ethics. And there does appear to be a great and ever-growing need for this form

of activity. At present we only have the
spiritual guidance of the clergy, or the
theories of scientific and philosophical
writers. On the one hand, we have the
ministers of religion, who claim that the
basis of their theory and practice is directly inspired and supranatural, and who
appeal to the highest human emotions,
namely, the religious feelings. The result is that, in the minds of those who are
to be influenced, the step from the loftiness of these thoughts and emotions to
the humbleness and minute multiplicity
of the ordinary acts of daily life is not
always readily or efficiently made ; while
the ministers of the inspired Word, speaking from their elevated position, are not
always credited by the plain and practical
listeners with experience of the needs and
demands of daily life, with being able to
guide them soundly and soberly within
this realm. On the other hand, students
of ethics have hitherto been too much
taken up with the purely theoretical principles of human action, more especially
with the broadest fundamental principles
of right and wrong, to have produced a

really practical guide to the conduct of
modern life. Even those writers on
ethics and sociology who claim to follow the inductive method have directed
their observation either towards the psy-
chology of man, or have examined him
historically or politically in large groups;
but they have never ventured, in their attempts at generalization, to attack the actual social and domestic ethics of the life
that is before us, entering into the duties
of definite professions and occupations, of
the employer to the employed, the master
to the servant, the housewife to the house-
hold, and other similar relations, the materials for the observation of which are
constantly before our eyes. Ethical inquiry seems chiefly to rotate round the
fundamental principles of transcendental-
ism and utilitarianism, egoism, altruism,
and other problems concerning the actual
or desirable motives to human action in
general. It may be that these complex
facts of simple daily life are as yet beyond
the reach of sound classification and scientific apprehension ; yet we cannot help
feeling their great practical use. How-

8

ever imperfect it may at first be, we cannot doubt the gain to scientific ethics of an attempt at exposition or codification of the principles and rules that guide or ought to guide our immediate conduct, based upon the careful and systematic observation of this daily life, if made by one trained in theoretical ethics, and otherwise qualified by sympathy, experience, and power of exposition to observe and to record the results of his observation in this sphere of ethical induction. Much that is now scattered among the writings of our essayists and in the religious and secular maxims of wise men, much of the writings of the casuists among the schoolmen, all brought together under the continuous and concentrated effort of one line of systematic thought, would then become the work of this modern ethician and sociologist. He would be a bold man who would undertake the task ; but, if at all well done, however far from presenting us with an absolute canon, it would undoubtedly be a great profit to mankind.

Between the priest, on the one hand,

and the theoretical ethician, on the other,
lies the activity in the sphere of sociology
and economics of writers like Ruskin.
He has, like Carlyle, whose disciple he
claims to be, boldly attacked the leading
vice of our age, which he would consider
to be the predominance of the mercenary
and commercial spirit, and a corresponding and consequent lowness of all our
ideals of life. Against this persistent vicious force nothing, however lofty, however holy, can hold its ground in the estimation of our majorities as a chief incentive to action. In his drastic manner he
has described this spirit of cupidity in the
most powerful terms, but in none more
pithily than in the passage in *Fors
Clavigera* relating to the benevolence
leading to railway enterprise : " The benevolence involved in the construction of
railways amounts exactly to this much
and no more—that if the British public
were informed that engineers were now
confident, after their practice in the Cenis
and St. Gothard tunnels, that they could
make a railway to hell, the British public would instantly invest in the concern

to any amount, and stop church building all over the country for fear of diminishing the dividends."

There can be no doubt that the ideals arising out of this predominant mercenary and commercial spirit have eaten at the marrow of many of the cardinal virtues of the past, of those demanded by the tasks of the present, and of those to be hoped for in order that we may create a progressive future. There are numberless people who consider themselves virtuous, and are recognized to be so by their neighbors, to whom the "getting on" ideal is ultimately the highest and leading motive of their life. Stories of exceeding parsimony, of the continued resignation of all other aims in life to the toilsome wrestling with untoward circumstance, until step by step men shall have advanced in the social scale and in wealth (or rather in wealth, and therefore in the social scale), at the cost of all other instincts of human life, that are repressed or extirpated in view of the one golden or gilt beacon-light of success, are, in the simplicity of a low moral standard, held up as instances of virtue worthy of emulation; while cringing public honor and consideration are based upon those signs and tokens which are impressed upon the metal by a mint recognized in the market-place. However much insincere cant there may often be in those who inveigh in a romantic spirit against the industrial life of modern times, comparing it with the life of the past, there does appear to me to be one symptom of disease marking our moral life in which we differ from other periods. This is perhaps the necessary concomitant of this period of transition in which we live. It is to be found in the want of clearness and singleness in our moral ideals with regard to the position of wealth, and the vacillation in our standard of moral approbation as professed and as followed by our ruling majorities. In more barbarous ages, or in the periods of chivalry, personal valor, however brutal in its results, was recognized as a virtue actuating the efforts and filling the life of the aspirant to honors. This the striving man honestly and fully believed to be good, and public esteem followed the realization of his virtuous effort.

In our highest moral moods we consider the " man's the gowd for a' that," and affect contempt for worldly goods and advancement, admiring the unworldly worker who substitutes the wealth of his own moral or intellectual life for the dross of riches; while the general public estimation, the public consciousness, as the Germans call it, still shows its approval of social consideration to the acquisition or possession of great wealth. This contradiction in our moral life is a feature distinguishing our age from those that have preceded us. The future will work out this problem, either by reconciliation of the two contending factors or by dissolution of the one or the other. It is against this idol that Ruskin hurls his most powerful invective, and he preaches with convincing strength and directness on the inner virtues which outshine the false light of the " getting on " ideal. He urges strongly and forcibly that the excellence of man does not depend upon the standing or scale of his profession or occupation, but upon his standing in his profession or occupation, whatever it may be; and he impresses upon every man the duty not to rise out of his profession into another supposedly higher one, but to make himself and his vocation better and higher by his noble efforts within its sphere. In his domestic life he has, before all, to find his house and fix his home, embellishing it and enlarging it, if needs be, but not shaking its moral foundations by an ever-present degrading hope of moving to a larger one. Whatever elements of communism or socialism there may be in Ruskin's writings, there is in this side of them a strong individualistic ground, in which the domestic life of the family is held by him to form one of the main pillars of social and political welfare. He also endeavors to define the province of woman in this well-regulated life; and though his manner here often has a touch of flowery condescension or unsimple simplicity, he assigns to her the deeply important function of the true woman and mother.

But his ethical teaching does not only

apply to the life of individuals ; he has also
turned his attention to the life of the nation as a whole, and in this national life
he has also pointed out the predominance
of the mercenary and commercial spirit.
He has shown what undue proportion and
engrossing interest are given to the mere
commercial and financial aspect of a
country ; and he has levelled his satire
and invective against the " period of un-
precedented prosperity" which formed the
staple of the speeches of statesmen touch-
ing upon the inner national life of a people. He has pointed out at what cost this
commercial prosperity may be bought,
not only to the advancement of the nation
as a whole, but to the citizens who produce this prosperity, in their moral and
intellectual as well as their physical life.
He has pointed out the vicious one-sided-
ness of the " political economists," whose
teachings form the only theoretical and
scientific groundwork for the practical
politician of the day, and he has denied
to these economists the designation of
political economists, distinguishing between political economy, which "con-

sists simply in the production, preservation, and distribution, at fittest time and
place, of useful and pleasurable things,"
. . . and mercantile economy, which sig-
nifies "the accumulation in the hands
of individuals of legal and moral claim
upon or power over the labor of others,
every such claim implying precisely as
much poverty and debt on one side as it
implies riches or right on the other." It
is not possible here, even if the writer
felt himself better qualified to enter upon
the discussion of definite problems of
political economy, to consider Ruskin's
views of co-operation, distribution, usury,
etc. Suffice it to say that he has been
one of the most powerful exponents of
the view now admitted into the most
sober and technical systems of political
economy: that this science or art is not
only concerned with the human motive
power and incentive to action which lies
in the immediate possessing and accu-
mulating instinct of man, and the blind
working of these forces in contending interests (a view which takes man in a
monstrous and one-sided aspect), but, as

it deals with the life of man, it must also
and primarily take into account, and
weigh and balance, as far as this is possible, the moral desires and needs of civilized human beings. In one word, he has
reconciled morality and economy, which
the old school of economists had di-
vorced.

It appears to be a natural phase of every young science in modern times, arising out of a desire to approach in method
the exact sciences, whether pure, such as
mathematics, or experimental, such as
chemistry and physics, to follow them in
their process of isolation of facts and phenomena, which no doubt facilitates the
exactness of their results and the sure-
ness of their advance. But at later phases
they will have to recognize that, where
with mathematical figures or with chem-
ical elements it is possible to isolate phenomena without impairing their essential
quality, as we rise to the scale of organic
life, and finally to human thoughts and
feelings, the isolation of phenomena does
not in the same way insure certainty of
scientific procedure, but, from the very

organic or moral nature of the factors with which the moral and historical sciences have to deal, alters, disfigures, and vitiates the essence of the phenomena thus isolated. The new life which has been given of late to the study of political and constitutional history may have led to this youthful exaggeration of so-called scientific method; and it may have to be recognized that, in dealing with the life of the past, the isolation of certain aspects within one period, such as the commercial life, or the foreign policy, or the party influence, when carried out in anything like the manner in which this is done with regard to the physical properties of solid or elastic bodies, may distort and disfigure facts and their relation. This is so because in the events of political life other varied interests, often of a very different nature, are inseparably interwoven with these broad currents of national action; and the pleasures of a prince or the intrigues of a woman, or, happily, a moral or religious idea, may modify and strengthen the course or divert the current of economical or foreign policy. To

assume that in political **economy moral**
considerations have not, and **will not have,**
a great regulating influence, **is as false to**
fact **as the views** of many doctrinaires,
who would entirely eliminate the moving
power **of** material interest, are Utopian.
There can be no doubt that the one-sided-
ness with which the old schools of economy proceeded in this direction **only had**
to lead **to a** reaction within the body **of**
the economists themselves, and **the** main
elements of this reaction are to be found
strongly put among all **the** writings of
men like Mill, whom Ruskin would re-
gard as one of the chief culprits in this
one-sided development of the study. And
though the works of many modern **writ-**
ers dealing directly **or** only **remotely**
with **such questions, such as the Comt-**
ists, **Kingsley,** Maurice, George Eliot, and
many others, have paved the way **for** this
healthy revulsion, Ruskin's merit **in** this
direction is incontestably **great, and** may
in the future grow in the recognition of
those who can look **more** dispassionately
upon his **exaggerations,** and **with more**
patience **upon his violent** petulance.

He has attacked the vicious fallacies in the very localities of their growth, the manufacturing centres of England, and has preached powerful sermons, which have undoubtedly had the effect of converting a few, of stimulating the moral fibre of many, and of causing many more to seek for some justification in the course they had before been following under the assumption that what they were doing was wholly right. He has shown to many what the real humanitarian spirit of Christian charity in its present form is, and how far it differed from their convenient belief that it was ordained by Providence that the circumstances of their lives should be so favorable to happiness, whereas those of their neighbors were so pregnant with misery. He has shaken the merchant and manufacturer out of their lazy and convenient dulness, in which their vocation had but the one goal of increasing their personal wealth, and has made them realize that they are also an integral member of organized society and the state, in which their function and duty in every stage of their vocation tend to ef-

fect the well-being of the whole organization. He has insisted upon the fact that
they have duties beyond the mere increase
of their personal wealth in the following
of their own vocation, as much as the soldier or the doctor or the teacher or the
priest, who could not consider their efforts to be exclusively directed towards the
acquisition of their pay or fee or salary.
He considers that the merchant and manufacturer have primarily the duty as masters to the servants whom they employ,
the master necessarily becoming in the
course of his business the overseer and
governor of large masses of men in the
most direct way, so that upon him falls
in a great part the responsibility for the
kind of life they lead. After this primary
duty is seen to, the main task of the merchant is to provide for the proper distribution of goods and wealth, and of the
manufacturer to produce the best and
most serviceable goods. Nay, according to
him, the manufacturer exists for the sake
of the workmen employed by him, and
is responsible to a considerable extent for
the bodies and souls of his employés, as

well as for the fabric they produce. The overstatement of this aspect of duty, which may be a literary quality, and may in its strong colors serve to attract attention,is nevertheless to my mind fatal in its influence, as, on the one hand, causing the votary who naturally would tend in this moral direction to become unbalanced in his enthusiasm, and unable efficiently to cope with the practical exigencies of life ; and on the other, from its exaggerated inaccuracy, strengthening the doubt of the hardened self-seeker, and giving him justification for a disbelief in such " unpractical ideals."

These injunctions concerning our mutual happiness and dignity, and of the furthering of the common social aims, ought certainly to be a negative guide in checking the positive current of individual interest, or they may even be raised into great positive ideals. But the self-interest of the merchant and manufacturer in gaining their own livelihood, and in increasing the possibilities of their own efficiency and happiness, limited by the due regard for public honesty and the welfare of those

with whom **they** are to co-operate **or to**
deal, ought to be recognized as an important and legitimate incentive to effort. It
might be said **that** this is self-evident, and
need not **be preached.** There may be **no**
necessity **to** preach **it, but we do** desire
that it be acknowledged and accredited
as being worthy of admission within the
recognized code of social ethics. The mis-
fortune has been and ever is, as it appears
to the writer, that the natural instincts of
self - preservation, physical, moral, and
æsthetic, are **taken** for granted as being
self-acting, **and only** requiring to be re-
pressed ; they are never raised within
the respectable company of moral tenets.
When they obtrude themselves upon the
attention, their existence and active power
being thus taken for **granted, a** disingen-
uous attempt is ever being made by well-
meaning preachers and moralists, either
to ignore them, or to hasten by them with
a sigh at the unfortunate necessity of
their existence and their claims, or to take
notice of them only by repressing or com-
bating them where they appear to assert
themselves too vigorously or stand in the

way of what is considered more worthy
of endeavor. We are untruthful to ourselves, and turn the whole of conduct into
most harmful dissonance, in thus ignor-
ing and shirking to deal with the natural
instincts and desires for self-preservation
and delectation as worthy to be admitted
into our rules of conduct; whereas we
ought to train them into their proper relation and proportion to our more altruistic duties, and ennoble them into a virtue
by the countenance morality gives them
as one of its tributary provinces, instead
of degrading them to the position of foreign and barbarous regions outside the
boundaries of the land of morality, with
a superadded falsehood of the feigned
negation of their existence.

So in the case of merchants and man-
ufacturers we ought to dwell and insist
upon the just motive of self-preservation
and delectation, but we ought to add the
other altruistic duties, now barely recognized at all in practice, because the really
active motive of individual gain has been
absolutely discountenanced by the high
moralists, and the people remain satisfied

9

with considering these vocations as outside the pale **of the** higher occupations,
with no laws whatever to govern them.

In the youthfulness of our moral awak-
ening we seem inclined to exaggerate the
claims of morality, as our predecessors
exaggerated the claims of utility ; and we
shall have to introduce into political **economy, as** well as into wider spheres, the
consideration of the playful and artistic
side of life, if we wish to be truthful to
fact, and if we would not bring about the
impoverishment and drought of the chief
springs **of** an elevated human existence,
We shall have to recognize that the elevating pleasures and delights, physical
and intellectual, in so far as they are **not**
essentially unsocial, and destroy or **stand**
in the **way** of common advancement, are
not only **(and** will **be for** incalculable
time) important motives to human effort,
but ought to be maintained as such, and
thus recognized within the province of all
serious consideration of social matters.

Nay, I would go further, without wishing to discuss the fundamental principles
of ethics, and maintain that the present

altruistic wave of humanitarianism which
we can trace in the lives of the good people among us is unbalancing the lives of
these earnest people, and may lead to
justified reactions which will retard sane
progress. Our duty to our neighbors,
and the duty of fully constituting ourselves as fit and useful members of organized communities, are insisted upon to
the exclusion of any claim to self-indul-
gence, without any acknowledgment of
a well-founded duty to self. And in the
ideal of these earnest people we have presented a picture which, in its fantastic
and hazy distortions of unreality, has a
profoundly tragic element. It is a world
in which the centrifugal efforts of good
men and women, restlessly active for the
pleasure and gratification of their neighbors, are directed into empty space, seeking for consistent bodies upon which they
are to spend their beneficent virtue; but
they never reach them, because each individual is surrounded by an impene-
trable circle of the same centrifugal force
of altruism, and the circles and forces
emanating from each personal centre

clash **and** absorb each other in the vain
endeavor **at** reaching the consistent centre of a human being that can feel and be
delighted, **and not** only act and distribute
blessings. **And** meanwhile the angels
that contemplate things human are weep-
ing bitter tears at the virtuous folly **of**
their human counterparts, who, **in the**
emulation of angelic sweetness, have mistaken the shadows for the essence, because of the glowing light of goodness
that prevails **above ;** and the ugly little
gnomes of hatred and selfishness, that dog
the steps of even good men, are chuckling
with suppressed titters of ironical laughter
at the general misery which unselfishness
can produce. Surely we can and **ought**
to train, or at least not to ignore **in false-**
hood, the more passive life of man's soul,
in which we can appreciate and feel delight in the good and great things that
others provide for us, and that we can
produce for ourselves and in ourselves.
And perhaps this appeal may come home
to the stern moralist if he realizes that
one great virtue, gratitude, will die of in-
anition without the grace of **receiving**

favors in this world, and that pride is likely to come where gratitude has no home.

Ruskin has taken a great part in bringing people to lead more unselfish lives, but he has also done much to give this one-sided tendency to moral activity, especially in his efforts to counteract the idea of play which happily still exists in England. To put it in the form of a pleonasm : If play loses its playfulness, it has lost its spirit and virtue; and if playful occupation is to be absorbed in the usefulness of its outcome, its own spirit and the salutary effect of training and feeding the passive side of mind is destroyed. The idea of finding our recreation in the production of some useful object thus in itself destroys the essence of play. Ruskin's opposition to the athletic pastimes and sports of England can be accounted for more readily in his own education than it can be justified in its effect. We do not mean to maintain that there are not many forms of it that in themselves are degrading in their influence, many that are unsocial in character, many, though

good in themselves, that have acciden-
tally developed into forms that under-
mine the moral health of the nation ; and
against these it is right that good men
should bring their influence to bear. But
in themselves they are one of the heir-
looms which the Englishmen of old have
handed down to their children, though
in many cases, from the exclusiveness of
the love bestowed upon them, they led to
a more or less brutal form of life. And
this heirloom ought to be cherished and
purified rather than impoverished and
destroyed. And if we examine into the
judgments of Ruskin and similar writers
on these matters, we shall find that they
have their own forms (though they may
be few) of play, in which they would indulge and have others indulge, and that
ultimately it depends upon their personal
predilections upon which form they would
put the signet of their moral approbation.
You will find some, whose physical vitality is low by nature or education (or its
want), who would only admit spiritual en-
joyments within the rightful recreations
of men and women. Others look with

extreme and self-satisfied displeasure and disapproval upon him who expends some of his time and substance upon the adornment of his person in the way of clothes that correspond to the modern standard of taste, and not to that of the ancient Greek, mediæval Frank, or the Norwegian Viking, whose dress he would like to revive; while they would feel justified in expending the same time and substance upon the binding of their books (apart from their contents) or upon the choice of their dinner-service. It is no doubt desirable to encourage good book-binders, but why not good tailors? Others, again, will rightly expend considerable sums upon their pictures and other works of art, yet will disapprove of the expenditure devoted to the acquisition of beautiful horses. They do not recognize the legitimate pleasure to be derived from the sight as well as the use of an animal, and as far as their action is concerned they would make the world the poorer by the extirpation of one of its most beautiful creations.

Perhaps it would be wise and just if

moralists, economists, social reformers, and political philosophers, of whatever shade of opinion, would **write in a** conspicuous place **in** their studies the monk's *memento **mori** :* **"Do not** make the world poorer, materially, intellectually, morally, and artistically, by anything your writings or preachings may lead men **to** do." And much of the wholesale **con**demnation of whole spheres of life and activity, in which one side or aspect has, from one point of view, been recognized **to be** bad, may be checked before **it** is hurled into the market-place.

A harmful outcome of the efforts, partly justified, of all such moralists as Ruskin and Carlyle in the England of to-day has been the stereotyping of differences in various sections **of the** social community. Among these I would except the most moderate and right-minded social reformer of the day, Matthew Arnold, whose influence must be, as it has been, **ultimately for** the world's good. They have created a marked antithesis between **on the one** side, a class of people who are supposed (or sometimes only suppose themselves) to have serious and engrossing moral aims in existence, and, on the other, those who apparently are carried on in the broad current of ordinary life without any consciousness, or at least any assertion, of higher social duties and moral ideals. The result is the creation of not only an unnatural and unjustifiable gulf between these two sections, which counteracts a proper fusion and mutual influencing of their currents, but it has led to a mutual contempt for one another, implying much self-glorification on either side, and it has confirmed and hardened each of the two sections in the peculiar vices and shortcomings to which it is prone. The thoughtless or fashionable man retaliates the moral haughtiness of the world-reformer by the assertion of his superiority in his own domain, expressed either by a vain contempt or at least apathetic desistence from intercourse; and he is met in the same way by the votaries of the other section. Occasionally it may happen that the extremist on the worldly side finds that his social opposite is not entirely devoid of sympathy with and ca-

pacity for the life which he considers a
desirable one; while the world-reformer
may realize that his fashionable friend is
neither a fool nor a bad man, and has
often thought, and acted up to his
thoughts, upon the problems and duties
of our life.

It thus appears to me that the real nature of recreation and its position in a
well-regulated life has not been properly
conceived by Ruskin, and it is, I believe,
owing to this want that he and other social reformers have somewhat overstated
the abuses inherent in the occupation of
the modern factory hand. It is to be
found in the powerful invective against
the thought-killing work of the mass of
our laboring classes — work in which
there is food for neither their intellectual
nor moral qualities. "You must either
make a tool of the creature or a man of
him," he says; "you cannot make both.
Men were not intended to work with the
accuracy of tools, to be precise and perfect in all their actions. If you will have
that precision out of them, and make their
fingers measure degrees like cog-wheels,

and their arms strike curves like compasses, you must inhumanize them. All the
energy of their spirit must be given to
make cogs and compasses of themselves.
All their attention and strength must go
to the accomplishment of the mean act.
The eye of the soul must be bent upon the
finger-point, and the soul's force must
feel all the invisible nerves that guide it,
ten hours a day, that it may not err from
its steady precision, and so soul and sight
be worn away, and the whole human being be lost at last—a heap of sawdust, so
far as its intellectual work in the world is
concerned ; saved only by its heart, which
cannot go into the forms of cogs and compasses, but extends, after the ten hours
are over, into fireside humanity. . . . It is
verily this degradation of the operative
into the machine which more than any
other evil of the times is leading the mass
of the nations everywhere into vain, inco-
herent destruction, struggling for a freedom of which they cannot explain the nature to themselves. . . . It is not that men
are ill-fed, but that they have no pleasure
in the work by which they make their

bread, and therefore look to wealth as the only means of pleasure. . . . We have much studied and much perfected of late the civilized invention of the division of labor, only we give it a false name. It is not, truly speaking, the labor that is divided, but the men—divided into mere segments of men—broken into small fragments and crumbs of life ; so that the little piece of intelligence that is left in a man is not enough to make a pin or a nail, but exhausts itself in making the point of a pin or the head of a nail. Now it is a good and desirable thing, truly, to make many pins in a day ; but if we could only see with what crystal sand their points were polished — sand of human soul, which has to be magnified before it can be discerned for what it is—we should think there might be some loss in it also. And the great cry that rises from all our manufacturing cities, louder than their furnace blast, is all in very deed for this — that we manufacture everything there except men."

And this misery, he says, can only be met "by a right understanding on the

part of all classes of what kinds of labor
are good for men, raising them and making them happy, by a determined sacrifice of such convenience or beauty or
cheapness as is to be got only by the
degradation of the workmen, and by
equally determined demand for the progress and results of healthy and ennobling
labor."

Now noble as is this appeal to our consideration of the dignity and happiness of
our fellow-men, and desirable as it may
be that we should ever bear these duties
in mind, I believe that there is much beg-
ging of the main question in these elo-
quent words, which may finally result in
fatal conclusions. The one important
question that will have to be considered
carefully, and cannot be met by rhetoric,
is the conception of *ennobling* and *degrading* work. In itself the attempt at
acquiring " the accuracy of tools, to be
precise and perfect in all their actions,"
is not degrading, however unattainable it
may be ; nor is it a " mean act " in itself
" to bend the eye of the soul upon the
finger-point, and the soul's force feel all

the invisible nerves that guide it, that it
may not err from its steady precision."
The true point perhaps really lies in the
"ten hours a day" of such occupation.
It is a question of degree, not of kind.
And if the amount of such work is deleterious to body and mind, it is against it
that the crusade ought to be waged. Nor
is there anything especially degrading in
the division of labor, if it also tends to
encourage, or at least not to destroy, the
possibility of the desirable division of
man's conscious life into work and positive effort and relaxation from work and
more passive recreation. It is practically
impossible, and perhaps ideally undesira-
ble, that work should be completely purified from the element of constraint and
continuous effort which distinguishes it
from play. Its real spiritual vitality and
ennobling incentive will ever be forth-
coming in the consciousness that the
immediate results of the effort meet the
need of society. Now if we are justified
in believing, as Ruskin does, that " it is a
good and desirable thing truly to make
many pins in a day," this consciousness

ought to prevent the laborer's moral effort
from tending towards his own degradation. Nay, the subjugation and discipline of his own faculties and instincts
for unbounded freedom would ever be a
type to him of the great and inspiriting
law which holds a perfectly organized society together, always provided that the
duration of this effort does not exceed the
limits of the proper conditions of physical and moral health, and that time and
opportunities for the culture of the rec-
reative side of his existence are offered.
There is hardly any occupation seriously
carried on which we can at present conceive of, that does not necessarily carry
with it that which in plain words is called
drudgery. The writer has known students and literary men who, in choosing
a vocation, preferred to the immediate
profession representative of their favorite
studies the drudgery of an office in the
civil service, where their business chiefly
consisted in adding up or controlling the
additions of the small salaries of soldiers
and officers in the army and navy. But
it may be added that this their daily

pursuit, which **at no** too great cost **gave**
them the feeling of having done their legitimate day's work, and furnished the
grateful prospect of subsequently prose-
cuting their favorite studies, was not too
long in duration of time ; and I may add
that it was the very mechanism **and**
thoughtlessness of their occupation which
constituted one element of their preference.

Without wishing to deny the existence
of much misery and of much that is
wrong among the factory hands, or the
general desirability of making work as
interesting as its efficient production will
admit, it appears to me that the main-
spring of Ruskin's opposition to factory
work lies in his opposition to the mechanical production, more especially steam-
manufactured goods. Let us at once
touch and meet the central doctrine by
stating a proposition which may, to
many, appear as evident as it undoubtedly is directly opposed to the chief views
expressed or implied **in most** of the writ-
ings of Ruskin and his allies and his dis-
ciples, namely : that if the best is good.

the second best is not necessarily bad;
and that if the production of the best is
in every way to be encouraged, this en-
couragement does not necessarily absorb
or exclude the desirability of fostering
the production of the second best, which is
not to be confounded with the second rate.
If a bronze repoussé or chased casket the
making of which took an artist-craftsman
five years of his most skilled labor could
only be bought by a petty prince four hundred years ago, and to-day perhaps only
by a national museum, then let this casket be made, and be made as well as
human hands guided by an inspired imagination can make it. But if, by the gal-
vano-plastic process, and by calling in the
aid of steam machinery, this masterpiece
can be reproduced at a trifling cost, so
that, where only the princeling could possess such a work four hundred years ago,
in hundreds of humble households the reproductions could adorn the room or sanc-
tify use by beauty, there can but be much
gain in every direction. And even if the
lines be not quite as precise and sharp in
the reproductions as they are in the origi-

10

nal, and the work is thus not best,* the
best still exists in the original, and what
so closely approaches it can only be elevating to the artistic taste of humble
people when constantly before their eyes ;
and the universal growth of public appreciation, needs, and demands in this direction, arising out of the distribution of such
second-best gems, will naturally lead to the
increased demand for the best originals.
Let us suppose (which is hardly conceiva-
ble) that the advance of mechanical skill
should enable us to dispense entirely with
human intelligent work, then it will be
right for such human activity to become
an interesting matter of historical contemplation and study, and this, to all but ro-
manticists, will justly be considered as a
blessing. No healthy mind really concerned about the welfare of humanity need
ever be appalled at the Promethean ad-

---

* The price and limited editions of Ruskin's books
have, in spite of all he may say, appeared to me a grave
contradiction, which is, however, to be accounted for by
the fallacious reasoning here pointed out. The adver-
tisement of limited editions of books and engravings, appear to me to mark an appeal to one of the most unsocial, and thus immoral, instincts of modern society.

vance in human skill. The reasoning of many of these Ruskinians, earnest men or shallow exquisites, in this half-moral, half-æsthetic realm, is misleading and insidious, because of the accompanying flavor of high morality and refinement. So, for instance, I have heard the antique system of casting bronze, known as *à cire perdu*, in which a mishap in the casting would destroy the wax model, and with it all the beauty, the result of so much inspired effort, commended as manifesting the high artistic earnestness and enthusiasm of the artists of old, as contrasted with the mercenary timidity or cowardice of modern artists, who, at best, would adopt means, while using the wax model, to assure the possibility of its reproduction. There was not only praise for the artistic enthusiasm of the artist of old, but blame to the modern artist for his desire to obviate, if possible, the absolute loss of his model. This is one of the worst forms of practical romanticism. Now if this process of casting *à cire perdu* does produce a more beautiful surface in the bronze work than any other form (which

it does), we ought by all means to possess
such works, and to revive the process.
But the loss of a beautiful statue by Dona-
tello or **Cellini** is a loss to the world ; and
it is an unsocial feeling which leads **us to**
admire less an **artist who** will strive to
discover, or will be gratified at **the discovery** of, some means of avoiding the
complete destruction of his ideas and labor as materialized **in** his model. The
perfecting and cheapening of reproduc-
tive art, whether good hand-made or mechanical copies, will invariably tend towards the increase for the demand of the
original artist's work in every direction.

There is at bottom an unsocial element
in this whole class of feelings among these
exquisites ; it is artistic pharisaism. **The**
main enemy in Ruskin's warfare against
modern industry is the steam - engine.
And it is here that his romanticism and
the unconscious workings of an unsocial
exclusiveness are the main motive powers
to **his** opposition. How much, from an
economical point of view, there may **be**
of truth in his idea that it would **be best,**
after using human hands, to exhaust **nat-**

ure's power of wind and water, and only
in the utmost extremity, after these have
been properly used, to turn to more artificial aids, I am unable to judge. But **we**
cannot help feeling that in his absolute
condemnation of the factory and railway
there is a strong element of romanticism,
which on the one hand wilfully blinds
its vision against the good that lies in one
great side of actual modern life, while it
is longingly directed towards a past which
to **the** people living in those ages was undoubtedly fraught with great evils and
miser**ies, and** which probably never existed as depicted by the romanticist. The
constant juxtaposition **of** the life **of** the
Swiss or the Tyrolese peasant with the
English farmer or laborer, giving rise **to**
a comparison in his words so much to the
detriment of the physical and spiritual
welfare of **the** modern toiler, strikes us as
being as far removed from the reality of
things as many romantic descriptions in
old-fashioned novels of the happiness of
the rural life of old, or the depiction, or
rather costume-painting, of the " *Salon
Tyroler* " is removed from truth. Hap-

piness and simplicity, if they really did
or do exist in these regions, may be confounded with animal restriction of wants
and brutal limitation of the means of sat-
isfying them.   And it is well for us carefully to question ourselves, when we com-
plain of the loss of picturesqueness which
modern improvements bring in their train,
whether unconsciously we are not speaking from gross selfishness, in which the
lives and happiness of living human beings are looked upon by us, in the consciousness of our intellectual or artistic
refinement, as scenes over which we smack
our lips as if we were reading a book or
seeing a play.   And as it is with the comparison of lives, so it may also be with
the comparison of institutions and things.
The preference which is given to the
windmill over the factory chimney may,
to a great extent, be purely romantic.   We
can conceive of a romantic knight some
centuries ago issuing from his castle gate
and complaining of the disfigurement to
the good scene of old caused by the suggestive structure with outspread wings
cutting the horizon line that bounded his

vast domain, as centuries hence we can
conceive of another romanticist who, longing with praise for the restoration of the
good old factory chimneys, complains of
the new structures erected to meet the
new wants of an advancing civilization.
The factory chimney is in itself, apart
from romantic associations, not necessarily more unbeautiful in line than the
windmill, and there is no reason why its
form should not be still more improved.

There is a truth strongly put by Ruskin
for which he would have gained more
universal recognition if the statements of
it had been more moderate and in conformity with fact, namely, the duty of
maintaining the land which we inhabit in
the conditions conducive to health, and
with the careful guarding and preservation of the natural and historical beauties,
which are, to omit all their spiritual qual-
ifications, real national possessions of the
highest economical value. To allow the
smoke from the chimneys to turn pure
air into pestilential miasmata, to see beautiful streams and rivers defiled, to witness
the most lovely and unique scenes ruth-

lessly robbed of their chief charms of natural beauty—these are losses which, if
they do bear comparison with actual industrial loss to individual members or
groups of the community, will outweigh
them heavily. The day may come when
one of the most important functions of
the government concerned with the in-
ternal affairs of a nation will be to secure
and guard the public lands for the purposes of national health and of national
delectation.

But when Ruskin complains that the
delightful silence which reigned in some
rural districts is now disturbed by the life
of industry, and that portions of Switzer-
land, which he and other kindred spirits
could once enjoy in comparative seclu-
sion are vulgarized by numbers of unedu-
cated tourists ; when he complains of the
very facility of approach to many of these
sacred haunts brought about by the railways, and the picnics which do not agree
with the exquisite musings of the solitary
votary of nature, we cannot help feeling
that this arises not only from a romantic
but from an essentially unsocial spirit.

There can be no doubt that our enjoyment must be impaired by the reduction of what stimulates our highest emotions to a commonplace; but we must willingly make this sacrifice when we consider the great gain accruing to hundreds or thousands where before it but reached units.

At bottom it is one and the same spirit of exclusiveness and exquisiteness which we before traced as influencing his views on other social and economical matters, and which we can trace at once in the intensity of admiration and the violence of denunciation in matters of art. And when in his followers, or in those influenced by him, this is coupled with dogmatism, we can see how this leads to the formation of a group of people whose belief in their own infallibility of taste and judgment is in potency only equalled by the narrowness of their vision. They believe and hold that they have found the true ideals of life, and that all others are idolatrous; that they possess the true touchstone of taste, and only admire what is best, and that all else is bad or vulgar.

And the worst is that apparent intensity
of feeling does not always insure absolute
sincerity of conviction; nay, that an unbalanced mind devoid of moderation is
likely to mar the trueness of its own
scales of veracity. And out of these conscious exquisites of mind and their ensu-
ing opposition to the current of ordinary
life there will naturally arise the desire
and the habit of manifesting distinctions
in outer appearance and conduct; and it
is thus that it may be in great part owing to this influence that the movement
which in its best sides has been productive of much good, but which has naturally and rapidly degenerated into the insincere forms that happily are dying the
death of innocent ridicule, the movement
the votaries of which have been called
æsthetes, has come to life. Though at the
beginning of this paper attention was
drawn to the fact that it was one of the
great merits of Ruskin to have successfully waged war against Bohemianism
among the artist community, his influence has tended to produce a far less
repulsive and obnoxious form of Bohe-

mianism. This is a very curious phe-
nomenon. For the essential characteristic of Bohemianism (and in this it is
related to romanticism) has ever been
negative, namely, its protest against existing ideals as manifested in the current
habits of life among the ruling majority.

Now it depends very much upon the
nature of the ideals and customs of this
ruling majority what form the Bohemianism of the day will take. The Philistine
of the German student, and that of the
dishevelled gentleman of the Latin Quar-
ter, and that of the modern æsthete, are
all very different people—nay, sometimes
they are diametrically opposed to one another. The modern English Bohemian
may be the Philistine *pur sang* in the estimation of the Bohemian of Heidelberg,
or of the streets abutting on the Paris
Pantheon. From a positive point of
view he certainly has a more moral or
artistic origin in his opposition to the
Philistine. There are three shadings
which we can distinguish among them,
all more or less degenerated practical
caricatures of the theories of their intel-

lectual parents. The first, deriving its
intellectual stimulus from Matthew **Arnold**, is more closely related in its antipa-
thies to the Continental prototype, especially that of Germany, inasmuch as the
Philistine here marks an uncultured *bour-
geois*, or the unintellectual country squire.
The second, arising out of Carlyle, **is the**
anti-Belgravian Bohemianism, and is more
directly opposed to the gilt world of fashion. And the third, the Ruskinian form,
comprising elements of both the previous
bodies, is anti-athletic, and draws its visi-
ble inspirations chiefly from **the** pictu-
resque side of art. The great good as
incentives that these extreme movements
were capable of doing, they have perhaps
already done, and **the** desirable part **of**
their vitality has probably spent itself.
Every Bohemian movement has the germs
of decay in itself, because of its essentially
negative nature. Very soon **the** ideals, in
so far as they were positive, **lose consis-**
tency; and only the dissenting forms **re-**
main. The mass of this community generally groups round some originator who
dissents from **strong inner motives ; but**

these **motives have not** their root in the
inner life of the followers, who tend towards formal exaggeration. And furthermore, the conventionality to which they
oppose themselves has one strong central
support, the very obtrusion of which the
Bohemian struggles **against,** namely, its
laws; while the opponents, on the other
hand, have not this to sustain **them, and**
thus readily run riot. **An** analogous case
is presented in the history of some religious sects of which **the founder may have
been a** fervent mystic; but the sect, as
such, has often degenerated **into** weakness, and **becomes a** malignant excres-
cency when constituted into an organized
body, making a rite and convention **of**
the very unconventionality of its spiritual founder, and the mystical fervor **has**
often degenerated into a frenzied luxuri-
ous dissipation, leading to the very opposite extreme of the spirit which moved
the leader. So here it would not be astonishing if æstheticism were gradually
to degenerate into a form of coarseness,
the very opposite of its refined origin.

The possible danger of Ruskin's influence, to which reference has just been made, far removed from the intended purport of his books, is not counteracted by a prominent tone of sobriety in his own works; nay, it is here that the dogmatic exquisite will find many instances of a prevailing spirit of narrow dogmatism. But in the life of this great man it can be accounted for and morally justified, which cannot be said of the unintelligent followers. It is the result of a life too much shut up in itself, and not sobered down by the constraint of fixed discipline, and widened out by continuous intercourse with people of equal calibre following different pursuits, and not necessarily responsive to his own views. It is a mind too much concerned with its own substance, revolving too much round one centre, and reflecting too much its own inner lights, rather than the direct lights from without. No doubt in his autobiography and in his works he dwells upon himself with an apparent impartiality most remarkable, and in so far unselfish; but still it is never free from egotism, and may be the height of it. He almost smacks his lips over himself as a thing to be studied, and appears at times touchingly humble and modest; but he is, after all, constantly busied about himself, and cannot forget it for work or in work. This is not only the case in *Præterita*, or to be noticed in the introduction of biographical matter into the *Fors* and many other of his writings, but smaller side lights show the same failing : as when he thinks it worth printing that a poem was written on New-Year's Day, 1828, in the *Queen of the Air;* when he thinks it proper to remark that he has a finer appreciation of nature than most people. His proffering remarks as to the extent he has worked upon a subject, how convinced he is of the truth, or the weight it has or ought to have, and the degree of earnest consideration it deserves—in short, the frequent mention of "I" where it should be "it"—all this is the result of a mind which, shut up in itself, drops into a kind of intellectual provincialism.

This exaggeration of the importance of one's own thoughts is often due to the

neglect of reading what others have written on the very subject of our thoughts.
Now a doubt must often have come to the
original student or writer as to whether it
can be of much advantage, if he has anything to say, to spend much time in **seeing** how others have said it, and to quote
their views and encumber his own with
foot-notes and the other customary forms
that characterize a scholar's work. **It**
may perhaps be better at times to work
straight on and write what one has to say,
for fear of otherwise never writing at all.
Still it **will** be found that the student becomes wider **in** following this old plan,
and generally without the loss of originality; he becomes maturer, clearer, **and**
more condensed. Besides this, there **is**
the question of honesty and moral regard
for previous work ; for it must be remem-
bered that general progress would be retarded if each student and writer would
have to begin anew, and **not** consider the
successful efforts of previous generations
and individuals. And **I** venture to think
that **if** Ruskin **had** followed this more,
and had been more **like** the German **pro-**

fessor he appears to despise, we should not have lost much of his originality, while I certainly hold that we should have had more system, more careful deliberation, and more moderation. There would have been fewer instances of dilettanteism in his works, and the great good that is in them would have stood out clearly, undimmed by the hasty exaggerations of a fatally facile pen and the immoderateness of a self-indulged imagination. But this painful tendency towards eccentricity, turning to habitual, and thus unconscious, exaggeration of mind and diction, is often fostered by the vicious influence of a selfish society, especially of idle and fashionable dilettanti. Just as (and here with more justification, perhaps) they will force a painter who has successfully drawn one kind of dog to paint nothing but this dog, so, seeing a new and striking side in a literary man, they will, urged by their unassuageable thirst for amusement, gradually force him to bring out that side in his ordinary intercourse, and thus turn originality into mannerism, into stereotyped epigrammatic exaggera-

11

tions, until they may succeed in producing the worst and most tragic form of a
hypocrite, namely, the unconscious actor
of a part, the dupe of a thumping insincere conscientiousness, of rude eccentricity. The result in many cases is the loss
of dignity in many good men of some
native power, who are often thus con-
verted into serious jesters by the selfish
requirements of a thoughtless society.
One of the greatest dangers to all genius
is that of being robbed of its vital strength
by velvety-pawed lion-hunters.

In the case of Ruskin, and in the case
of his master in some departments, Carlyle, the prevalence of the relentless, exaggerated, denunciatory frame of mind
and form of expression has often beguiled
them away from the noble course of sober and conscientious search after truth,
absorbing much of the energies that are
painfully needed to reduce to order the
tangled web of the innumerable facts
that crowd round the narrow gateways
of conclusions justified by truth. It has
kept them from curbing subjective impulses, strong desires and passions and

prejudices, and of bending their energies to the service of the stern-browed
goddess; it has lured them on to the
riotous chase of the mænad whom they
mistake for a muse. The prophetic denunciatory tone in its resounding flow
may prove to be an easy means of shirking and avoiding the great task of declar-
ing to men the hard-won truths that are
announced in simple, diffident, nay, halt-
ing words, but still penetrate and endure
in their far-reaching quality of sound.
And ultimately the result upon such men
themselves, and a baneful influence upon
all who come within the circle of their
power, is a general blunting of the keen
edge of what we must call intellectual
morality, that moral and mental habit
which makes it impossible for any man
to state as an undoubted fact whatever he
has not conscientiously tested and examined in all its bearings.

There is nothing we would plead for
more earnestly than moderation in matters intellectual. We are often told that
exaggeration is demanded to reach and
move the masses, in order that a general

truth might become practically effectual
and leave the spheres of pure thought.
We are informed that minute and careful
balancing of truth finds its place in the
silent study; but that, when we go out
into the market-place and thoroughfares
of actual life, we need direct and forcible
statements, figures of prophets and movers
of men who stand out strongly as types
of the one idea which they incorporate
—comparative coarseness of intellectual
fibre and passionate boldness of expression. Luther moved men, we are told,
not Melancthon and the humanists. It
has almost become a commonplace to
say: not the sober student, but the prophetic enthusiast is required to effect great
changes in the world's history. I will not
attempt here to answer the question
whether, if we look into history carefully,
we shall not find that, after all, the moderate student was not more efficient in
turning the world's current into lasting
and beneficent channels than the violent
enthusiast, and that the latter really only
became influential when he made himself
the mouth-piece of the former. I should

further suggest the question whether each exaggerated movement does not bring with it a corresponding reaction, corresponding in strength to the degree of exaggeration, and acting, in the long-run, as a retarding force to human progress, quite out of proportion to any temporary gain apparent at the time of the exaggeration ? If we must needs have strong preaching, then there is one topic for the moralist and world-reformer in which exaggeration is least likely to be harmful— the gospel of Sanity and Moderation.

Ruskin has often allowed his feelings to run counter to the workings and injunctions of this higher duty. In the preface to the *Seven Lamps* there are " cases in which men feel too keenly to be silent, and perhaps too strongly to be wrong ;" he ought to have guarded most jealously against the strong feelings as often making it more probable that we may go wrong. The use of superlative adjectives condemning or praising, with him and with Carlyle, points to the same bluntness of intellectual morality. One thing or work is wholly " bad," another at once all that is " good."

He passes judgment not only upon all forms of art, but upon the works of great and sober men of science, on the problems of these departments of science themselves, whether it be the works of an Agassiz or of a Darwin, the purport of whose work he had never trained himself to realize. Such exaggerations may, alas, from a literary point of view appear to be innocent, but in their effect they certainly are not. He will, for instance, in *Præterita* II., page 298, tell us, with the emphatic terms of a convinced authority, speaking of Sydney Smith's *Elementary Sketches on Moral Philosophy*, that " they contain in the simplest terms every final truth which any rational mortal needs to learn on this subject." We must ask what right his reading of that vast subject called philosophy has given him to pass judgment in any way upon it. And so, in almost every chapter of all his books, we cannot help feeling that this is a positive blemish, the influence of which cannot be good ; and we turn with pure gratitude to his descriptive passages, where there is no scope for this intellectual vice, and where the good that is in him has brought forth fruit that will be the delight and profit of all the ages in which the English language is read. If, as far as intellectual example is concerned, we turn from the prophetic and denunciatory violence of Carlyle and Ruskin to the charitable and unselfish statement of a great continuous effort in a long laborious life, beautiful as it is simple, we cannot help feeling that, besides the results of the actual research of Charles Darwin, his literary and scientific example as a writer can but have a lasting and elevating influence upon the minds of all those who read him for generations to come. No amount of denunciatory sermons can replace the unconscious preaching contained within the work and its results of the student who has honestly mastered a subject, however narrow its range. This is the highest form of preaching, if only for the supreme effect, the suppression of impulse and passion for an end that has no immediate bearing upon our own interests, and does not flatter 'our vanity in the elevation of our own position to that of a direct teacher or

chastiser of foolish humanity, and above
all in the jealous custody and possible refinement of our feeling for truth.* It appears to me one of the greatest blemishes
in the work of men like Ruskin and Carlyle that, however high the position they
may themselves assign to truth in their
moral scales, the actual tenor of their
work has counteracted rather than favor-
ed this desirable consummation. Bearing this in mind, we can recognize the
good that is in Ruskin's work, and there
will be enough of merit remaining to
make him one of the great benefactors of
mankind.

* The development of this intellectual morality **as a**
habit in individuals, and as a tradition in a **nation and in**
an age, is intimately connected with practical **morality**
and truthfulness ; and **there appears to me to be a strong**
moral and disciplinary bearing **in the** methods of **research**
as applied to the natural sciences within our days, to
which Charles **Darwin has** chiefly contributed. It is
true, the inductive method was recommended **by** Bacon
and insisted upon by Hume ; but it has only become a
fact in Darwin ; and through his efforts and those **of** his
numerous followers and co-operators the general habit of
mind which is developed **by their** methods of work has
not only penetrated **into other regions of** thought and
study, but it is modifying and raising our general **stand-**
ard of truth even in our practical daily life.

V

MR. RUSKIN AND THE SPORTS AND PAS-
TIMES OF ENGLAND

THE field-sports and pastimes of England play so important a part in the life
of the English people, and might so
well serve as an example to other nations, that I do not think the most serious thought we may spend upon them
wasted. Nay, I hold that a serious treatment of the subject is called for the more,
as the weight of personality and earnestness of moral purpose which writers and
thinkers such as Mr. Ruskin have thrown
into the scales may cause the balance to
fall on what to my mind is the wrong and
harmful side.

The first fallacy seems to me to consist
in the view taken by Mr. Ruskin and his
followers that these sports are essentially characteristic of the upper or leisured

classes of England, as opposed to the
working - classes, and in so far act as a
severing element. Now, in opposition to
this view, I strongly hold that these institutions have occupied a conspicuous
place in the history of the English people
as a uniting element: that they have
brought the people together, have given
a tangible unity of character to the English
nation, and have been one of the most
important factors in hitherto mitigating
the antagonisms of class feeling which,
from other conditions of life, might
have become most marked and stereotyped.

In the first place, I deny that sport in
England is in any way limited to the upper or leisure classes, in contradistinction
to the working - classes. There may be
and there no doubt are some men who
do no work (though both in England and
America these are not always men who
take to sport) ; there are no doubt those
who only live to hunt, and do not hunt
to live. But it is unfair to take this exaggerated type as the centre of attack
upon the institution as a whole.

To begin with young people, both in
the schools and in the universities the
athlete and the sportsman are very frequently the reading men who work hard-
est. This is markedly the case in the
universities with regard to rowing men,
cricketers, and foot-ball players. No
doubt, both in schools and universities,
many instances may be found in which
the games have been abnormally developed and have received excessive consideration. But in every institution, however
good and noble its purpose, exaggerations
and abnormalities can always be pointed
out.

In the later periods of men's lives, when
they have left the schools or the universities, I would again maintain that the
majority of the men who play cricket or
foot-ball, who row, who shoot, or fish, who
climb the Alps, and even those who hunt,
are busy men, hard workers in their several vocations. Nothing but actual sta-
tistics could absolutely prove the one or
the other assertion. But, from my own
experience and the means I have of esti-
mating the numbers, I would challenge

those who assert the contrary to prove their statement.

I have said "even those who hunt," for, from the nature of this sport, it would appear that it might readily be limited to the few who could devote a considerable portion of their time and energies to ride in pursuit of the fox. Among a few packs in the midland counties of England, where, from the nature of this grass country and its fences, hunting is exceptionally good, while requiring the most expensive mounts to see a good day's sport, there may be a large proportion of men whose means are so ample that they would not be forced in any way to exert themselves to provide for their maintenance. But even there, with these few packs of hounds, I do not think there is a large proportion of men whose whole time is spent in seeking for personal distraction and enjoyment, and who have not some definite, serious vocation in life. But when we leave these packs, in considerably over a hundred hunts scattered over England alone, the case is a very different one. We have an adequate picture of national life, and perhaps national life at its best. Many classes are here represented. There may be a peer or two, a few squires, farmers, doctors, lawyers, tradesmen, the butcher and baker on his horse, boys and girls on their ponies, old men and young men—and all mixing in a spirit of comradeship and good - fellowship, with the health - giving life of a day in the open country on horseback (and sometimes off it), with no thought of the rivalry of clashing interests in the great greed of gain. A foreigner coming to England cannot understand this. His question is: "Who has invited these people?" With him some great nobleman would for any similar function have invited a few select guests, and admission into this magic circle would at once confer social distinction. But here is a real national holiday, and whoever desires to do so can join in the sport, and will be properly treated by all other sportsmen, provided he behaves properly. The rebuke administered to the successful London tailor who had taken to hunting will illustrate the spirit in which any attempt at establishing exclusiveness is met.

This sportsman - tailor was riding home after a day's hunt with a well - known duke, and after commenting upon the day's sport, he remarked to his noble companion that the company was rather mixed. " You wouldn't have them all tailors, would you?" was the duke's reply.

We must feel that in this respect the conditions of "shooting" in England are unfavorable.

In the first place, from the nature of land - tenure and of the distribution of game, the opportunities of shooting are limited to a great extent to people of considerable wealth. It is more and more becoming the sport of the rich in this densely populated country. Then it differs from hunting and most sports and games in that only a limited number of people or "guns" can take part in any shooting - party; and such parties are thus closely defined and distinct from the less fortunate lovers of sport. And, finally, considerable ill - feeling has been engendered, on the one hand, by the strict preserving of whole districts and the quarrels to which it leads; on the other hand, by the numerous cases of severe judgments passed by magistrates upon the offenders against the game-laws.

Against these facts it may be urged that the rich landlord does not shoot in solitary state, but that he invites a number of people who could not afford to keep up preserves themselves, representing the various classes and occupations ; that recent legislation concerning "hares or rabbits" has given extensive rights to the tenant-farmer ; and that there would very soon be no game at all in England if there were not those to preserve it.

In spite of what may be said, the fact remains that this form of sport is more likely to act as a severing element than the other games and sports, and that it certainly does not in the same way tend to unite the classes. Still the conditions are accidental and not essential to the sport itself.

But taking the sports and pastimes as a whole I am convinced of their influence in binding the classes together rather than severing them. The fact that England is and has been more consistently and continuously aristocratic in constitution than any other country **in** Europe, and at the same time in its actual national character **in** many aspects more democratic, is, I maintain, in great part due to the existence **of these** games and **pastimes.** They provide for the people as a whole a common language and a field of mutual understanding and sympathy, so that **the aristocrat** has not become estranged from **the** simple laboring man to the same degree **as in Germany. The** British laborer, the **artisan,** the villager, the tradesman, the **soldier** and sailor, have all become infused **with** this modern survival of chivalry, which is to a great degree wanting, say in the German, his nearest **in kin** in Europe. The village cricket-field, the football match, **the** rowing **race,** the games in the regiments and among the crews and **officers of a** man-of-war, the hunting-field—all these are places where the different classes have **met** in common spirit **and** with comparative freedom and intimacy. **When** the manifestations of **physical** strength and **skill** become the main central object of exertion, evoking inter-

est and bringing prestige, there is no
chance to obtrude or to maintain the set
differences of class. The village hobble-
dehoy who plays well in a good match
becomes a hero for the day along with
the young peer, the private soldier no
less than his officer, and the butcher who
"rides straight" as well as the master of
hounds. And so it is in every sphere of
this healthy physical life.

Without these institutions, what would
the English schools be? The danger that
the poison of snobbishness which ema-
nates from such social centres as London
might vitiate the early impressionable nature of boys is very great. But, though
the exaggeration of athleticism may create a school-snobbishness of its own, still
this new physical criterion of estimation
established among boys is a healthy coun-
teractant in early youth to the effects of a
worldly society in after life. The same
applies to the universities in which the
range of these causes of distinction is
healthily widened by deeper and more
lasting objects of estimation. But all
these influences join to counteract the

stereotyping of social classes based **upon** wealth or other adventitious **grounds.** Outside **England** the fact can hardly be realized that in the schools there are football matches between **the masters and the** pupils, that **in the** colleges of **the great** universities there **are** matches between the members and " dons" of a college and the college servants. And surely we need not insist upon the fact that such intercourse, though not affecting the discipline necessary for the practical purposes of life, **is most** salutary **in** bringing together **and** in effecting a healthy *rapprochement* among **these** distinct bodies of men.

No two Englishmen, though they be of the opposite poles in **the** social world, need be **at a** loss **to find a common** ground **of** conversation if **they both** take interest **in** some form of **sport.** And it would be difficult **to** find **an** Englishman, **to** whatever class he may belong, who, from bicycle-riding, **or foot-ball, or row-** ing, or sailing, or fishing, **or hunting on-** ward, does not **take** some interest **in one or** the other of these athletic games.

Of course national life would **be still**

more perfect if the highly-educated man could converse with the country-laborer about the latest literary publication or the different divisions of intellectual work. In this the Germans, from the long tradition of their school education, are far ahead of the English. The writer can remember with what pleased surprise he listened to the landlord of a small inn of a remote hamlet in the Black Forest, when he visited this district on a tramp during his student days at a German university. This peasant (for such he was) at once asked us whether we belonged to the juridical, philosophical, or theological faculties, or whether we were students of medicine. He had a clear notion of the distinctions between the different lines of university study, and fully realized the theoretical aspect and worth of higher scientific pursuits. One could hardly meet with such a man in England. But in Germany there would be no bond of sympathy in that region of life and interest to which sport belongs. While acknowledging that the presence of both elements of union is necessary for a per-

fect national life, we must at the same
time rejoice that in England we can at
least point to the existence of one.

The Germans do not possess this spirit
on which chivalry rests: the emotional
and physical sympathy arising out of the
near intercourse of men joined together
by the free and expansive spirit of **physical play**. And this implies a communion
and acquaintance which common intellectual interests cannot supply. We can sym-
pathize with the Irish **officer** in an English regiment, **who,** on being reproached
by his brother officers for talking volubly
and at length with an Irish visitor, whereas
he did not converse freely with them, **an-**
swered : "Sure, and he knew a **hoss that**
I was acquointed with." **The** Oriental,
when **he wishes to express the** fact **that
he knows a** man intimately, says, "I have
travelled with him." We might with the
same object say, "He was in the eleven
with me."

We can hardly overestimate the train-
ing which those **who** fill the humbler
walks of life in the country **in** England
have gained from this **intercourse with**

those who have had better opportunities
for refined training. It has improved their
manners, it has increased their pluck and
self - control, it has refined their social
feeling. Nay, the "professionals" in England, those who have made a business of
games, especially cricket, have often over-
come the dangers which attend such exclusive occupation, and have maintained
a higher and more refined standard of
life by the aid of their constant associa-
tion with men of high and noble character
who cultivate these games in England.

Even horse-racing has furnished a bond
of sympathy between all classes of the
people in England and Ireland. No one
could deplore more the base mercenary
element of betting, which has become at
times almost indissolubly connected with
this sport. It is so great an evil as to
counterbalance all the good that the institution itself undoubtedly possesses; and
one would like to see it swept away, to
avoid the accidental evil which has penetrated into the very heart of its life. But
as regards the interest in the racing itself,
one need but go to the Derby or to

Punchestown in Ireland to see what a national binding element it is.

I feel sure that the most patriotic and far-sighted of the Germans, their present emperor at the head, would make any sacrifice, if they could but create the same intense interest in the whole of the German people as now moves England when the sixteen representatives of the two great universities vie with one another in their annual boat-race.

Surely these institutions do not keep the classes asunder. The wrong comes, and the hateful side is turned uppermost, when men cultivate these sports to gain social distinction by them, and to impress their less fortunate neighbors with the advantages which material accidents have placed in their own way. I maintain that these are not real sportsmen, as little as the long-haired æsthete who consciously draws a distinction between himself and the less fortunate Philistine is a real lover of art.

It is wrong to create artificial antagonisms and to counteract what is, when soberly and impartially considered, one of the greatest boons in these not too bright times of ours.

And if now we consider the influence of these institutions upon the individual man in maintaining and increasing physical and moral health of normal life, I would here again hold them to be the greatest boon to England. When Jorrocks calls hunting: " The sport of kings, the image of war without its guilt, and only five-and-twenty per cent. of its danger," the jesting tone cannot wholly hide the deep truth that lies beneath. These games and sports cultivate the physical side of our soul, our pluck, power of emotiveness and vigor of impulse, together with the potency of self-control. We cannot conceive of a perfect man without physical courage. It is true the question may be asked whether, by directing our minds and bodies into other channels that have no taint of the savageness of the prehistoric man, we cannot equally fortify this impulse to action and feeling and thought. It is true it may require as great an expenditure of will-power, of self-control, of pluck, or whatever else we might call it, to check the impulse of irritation in our ordinary life and intercourse, or to force ourselves to do a small, humble piece of work, when indolence drags us the other way, as it requires to scale a high mountain or to face a stiff fence in the hunting-field. But I do not think that in these complex calls upon our inner nervous system which ordinary civilized life in towns and rooms brings to us we obtain so pure and direct a training of the side of our nature which corresponds to physical courage as in those occupations which are purely and directly the outcome of undepraved physical vitality.

We do not wish to return to the prehistoric savage. We have certainly "evolved" out of those primary conditions of man's soul, as we have "evolved" out of those conditions of life. But, "evolve" as much as we may, and as high as we can, out of the stage of savage man, we cannot conceive, within appreciable time, our "evolving" away from the conditions of *man*. And as yet, in all our conceptions of the most perfect man—

even for the **remote** future—the element
of physical courage, of θυμος, as Plato
would call it, is an essential **factor.** And
I maintain emphatically that there **is no**
sphere in which these virtues can be more
efficiently and beneficially cultivated and
fostered than in the **exercise of games**
and sports. The vicious **impulse of an**-
tagonism, which, from the **instinct of**
self-preservation, seems to **be imbedded**
in man, which led to the fight **and the**
slaughter of **his** fellow-men; the almost
savage predominance of other emotions
and passions which, though blended with
our highest and noblest impulses, may destroy their **nobility** and bring **misery upon**
our fellow-beings—these are led **into more**
harmless channels, are subdued **to their**
right and healthy measure, and, without
the barren attempts at extirpation which
bring disease to the soul's life, **they are**
subordinated, as parts of an organic **ex-**
istence, to the highest aim of the life of
every human being.

It is especially the intellectual man, the
brain-worker, who often neglects this side
of his life **until the** prevailing *nevrose*

eats at the heart of his soul's forces. He
it is whom we ought to meet in the hunting-field, on the river, at cricket and foot-
ball. And, fortunately, in no country more
than in England are these men votaries
of these noble pastimes. But it is not only
in this quasi-utilitarian spirit, in which we
regard these forms of play simply as means
to fit us the better for the more serious
tasks of life, that I wish to view them:
they are a direct end in themselves. We
do not wish to join the "liver brigade"
who ride in the park in the morning to
regulate their digestion. We wish to see
young and healthy people riding for the
pleasure of riding, and not only to fit them
for work. Mr. Ruskin has in one passage
entered into the spirit and the nature of
play when, in the *Crown of Wild Olive*,
page 20, he says : " First, then, of the distinction between the classes who work
and the classes who play. Of course we
must agree upon a definition of these
terms—work and play—before going further. Now, roughly, not with vain sub-
tlety of definition, but for plain use of
the words, 'play' is an exertion of body

or mind, made to please ourselves, and
with no determined end ; and work is a
thing done because it ought to be done,
and with a determined end. You play, as
you call it, at cricket, for instance. That
is as hard work as anything else ; but it
amuses you, and it has no result but the
amusement. If it were done as an ordered
form of exercise, for health's sake, it would
become work directly. So, in like manner, whatever we do to please ourselves,
and only for the sake of the pleasure, not
for an ultimate object, is 'play,' the 'pleasing thing,' not the useful thing. Play may
be useful in a secondary sense (nothing is
indeed more useful or necessary); but the
use of it depends on its being spontane-
ous."

The general tenor, however, of his remarks upon play, especially the field
sports, is in direct opposition to this
view. When, for instance, in another
passage in the *Fors*, he says that, "if instead of taking the quantity of exercise
made necessary to their bodies by God,
they take it in hunting or shooting, they
become ignorant, irreligious, and finally

insane, and seek to live by fighting as well as by hunting; **whence the** type of Nimrod in the **circle** of the Hell **towers** which I desire you to study in Dante."

He objects **to** these games on **the** ground of waste, and would like to **see** the energy and money now spent in them turned into more immediately productive channels. It is especially against hunting and shooting that his opposition is aroused. Thus he says again, in the *Fors*, "Our next English game (he has been speaking of money-making **as** the first game), however, hunting and shooting, is **costly** altogether, and how much we **are** fined for it annually in land, horses, gamekeepers, and game-laws, and all else that accompanies that beautiful **and special** English **game, I will** not endeavor **to** count **now : but not** only that, except for **exercise, this** is not merely a useless game, **but** a deadly one to all connected with it. . . ."

And, again, his letter on the subject of fox-hunting, to **the** *Daily Telegraph*, **of** London, republished in the *Arrows of the Chase*, p. 118 : "Reprobation of fox-hunt-

ing on the ground of cruelty to the fox is
entirely futile. More pain is caused to
the draught-horses of London in an hour
by avariciously overloading them than to
all the foxes in England by the hunts of
the year; and the rending of body and
heart in human death, caused by neglect,
in our country cottages, in any one winter, could not be equalled by the death-
pangs of any quantity of foxes.

"The real evils of fox-hunting are that
it wastes the time, misapplies the energy,
exhausts the wealth, narrows the capacity,
debases the taste, and abates the honor
of the upper classes of this country; and,
instead of keeping, as your correspondent
'Forester' supposes, 'thousands from the
workhouse,' it sends thousands of the
poor both there and into the grave.

"The athletic training given by fox-
hunting is excellent; and such training
is vitally necessary to the upper classes.
But it ought always to be in real service
to their country; in personal agricultural
labor at the head of their tenantry, and
in extending English life and dominion
in waste regions against the adverse pow-

ers of nature. Let them become Captains of Emigration, hunt down the foxes that spoil the Vineyard of the World, and keep their eyes on the leading hound in Packs of Men."

Mr. Ruskin's practical experiment while he was at Oxford to direct the surplus energy of healthy men into what he considered the proper channels is well known. He endeavored to persuade the serious-minded young students of Oxford that, instead of expending their energies in games, they should find their physical amusement in making roads and doing other manifestly useful tasks in the open air.

Now I maintain that these views are based upon the fundamental misunderstanding of the nature of play—of its position in the economical as well as generally in the ethical life of the healthy civilized man of modern times—a misunderstanding strange in view of the correct definition of play quoted above.

From an economical point of view, I claim that the needs which the games supply are for us as fundamental as any

of the other goods of life. Nor do I see
how their cessation throughout a country
like England could be in any way a reme-
dy for the economical diseases, the causes
of which lie much deeper, and cannot be
palliated by their disuse. Even if it could
be shown that by the complete destruction of these institutions an appreciable
amount of sustenance or comfort could
be distributed among all the individual
members of a community, I should say
that our community, or country, or age
would, as a whole, be impoverished in the
resources of its life. If we were to turn
all our capital and efforts into the direction of producing wheat and potatoes,
there is no doubt we might produce more
wheat and potatoes; but what would become of the flower-gardens and the wild-
flowers, so injurious to the farmer's hay
crop, but for the preservation of which
Mr. Ruskin is such a warm advocate. He
likes flower-gardens, others like fox-hunting, others like both; and the world is the
richer for their tastes. He is wrong when
he makes the absurd and unfair comparison between the life suggested by the

picture of a mediæval Madonna and a
caricatured account of modern sport, and
when he says (*Fors*, letter xxiv.) : "Of
course all this is quite natural to a sport-
ing people who have learned to like the
smell of gunpowder, sulphur, gas-tar, better than that of violets and thyme.   But,
putting the baby-poisoning, pigeon-shooting, and rabbit-shooting of to-day in comparison with the pleasures of the German
Madonna and her simple company, and
of Chaucer and his carolling company,"
etc., etc.   If he wishes to inveigh against
pigeon-shooting or unsportsmanlike rabbit-shooting, let him do it ; or if he wishes
to praise the simplicity of life suggested
by these mediæval types, he can do it eloquently.   But why indulge in this un-
called - for and distorting juxtaposition
and contrast!   He is thus wrong, both
theoretically and practically, when he puts
in glaring opposition the misery and the
material wants of the destitute ; when,
after giving a harrowing picture of the
misery in poor London, he says, "And
the double and treble horror of all this,
note you well, is that not only the tennis-

playing and railroad - flying public trip round the outskirts of it," etc., etc.

If the very foundations of our whole economical and social life are to be altered so as to right the wrongs and to equalize the cruel inequalities in our midst, then the right-minded among us will be prepared for this, and will hail with joy any reforms which would bring justice into the world. But meanwhile let us not impoverish the world and lower our ideals of perfect life, moral, intellectual, and physical. The world without "tennis" would be the poorer for it.

If such reasoning is fallacious economically, it is still more so ethically and as regards the proper understanding of the essential nature of play. Play is to our physical life what art is to our intellectual and moral life. Both arise out of the healthy vigor of human society that has risen beyond the stage of animal instincts and barbarity. When man's thoughts and exertions are not merely bent upon self-preservation and production of the mere necessaries for physical subsistence, his healthy mind and his healthy body turn

to spheres where there is exertion (not
passive vegetating existence) which re-
freshes and elevates, and has no ulterior
object. Active exertion, in which action
itself becomes the end, without further re-
flection and remote considerations, which
would counteract and vitiate the reviving
influence of such activity—this leads to
art and to play. The mind revels in the
contemplation of the beauties of nature
or in a picture, or a statue, or a poem, or
a drama, or a symphony, or a beautiful
tower, as the body revels in a brisk walk
in the country, in a swift ride on a bicycle,
in a fast pull on the river, in a good game
of cricket, of base-ball, of foot-ball, or a
good run across country. As modern civilized society has evolved art, and needs
it, as the civilized and properly educated
man and woman require the satisfaction
of the æsthetic side of their soul, in order
that it shall be healthy ; so civilized life
has developed those games and sports,
and the healthy man and woman require
the satisfaction of their physical vitality
in these directions, in order that they may
remain sound and normal beings. And,

as Mr. Ruskin himself has recognized, to
add an ulterior aim of utility to such efforts destroys the very essential nature of
these acts. Road - making, excepting in
the first few attempts, when it is looked
upon as a " joke," cannot satisfy that side
of our nature which makes for play.

Mr. Ruskin's opposition to these games
and sports can, I believe, be easily ex-
plained in him : they come, on the one
hand, from what I have called his ethical
bias, on the other hand from his romanticism. To our mind his ethical bias has
even vitiated his proper conception of art.
Still more can we feel how his earnest
sympathy with men of all ranks, his deep
pity for misery, his passionate resentment
of the wrongs which strike great classes
of men, should have made him overshoot
the mark and ignore the good which lies
in so simple a phase of human existence
as is covered by the idea of play. And it
is always an ungracious task to plead for
what may appear trite in the light of the
great absorbing issues of a lofty human
life, to sound the gentle pipe when there
is the blast of the trumpet in our ears, to

hang one's simple picture of a country lane in the morning mist, green and gray and light blue, beside the great imagery of the setting sun in all his golden, crimson, purple glory, or beside the picture of a battle-scene with a blood-red background to it. But from the point of view of completeness, normality, and health of social life, the claims of the one have the same right as those of the other.

Mr. Ruskin's romanticism shows itself in his treatment of sport, especially in the manner in which he approaches some forms of it. So, for instance, in *Fors*, vol. i., p. 119, he speaks of riding and sailing: " You little know how much is implied in the two conditions of boys' education that I gave you in my last letter—that they shall all learn either to ride or sail: nor by what constancy of law the power of highest discipline and honor is vested by nature in the two chivalries—of the Horse and the Wave. Both are significative of the right command of man over his own passions; but they teach, further, the strange mystery of relation that exists

between his soul and the wild natural elements on the one hand and the wild lower
animals on the other."

He then dwells upon the gentleness of
chivalry, and quotes the *Iliad* for the conception of the horse, there manifested in
the sorrow of the divine horses at the
death of Patroclus. "Is not that a pret-
tier notion (p. 120) of horses than you will
get from your betting English chivalry on
the Derby day? We will have, please
Heaven, some riding, not as jockeys ride,
and some sailing, not as pots and kettles
sail, once more on English land and sea;
and out of both, kindled yet again, the
chivalry of heart of the Knight of Athens,
and Eques of Rome, and Ritter of Germany, and Chevalier of France, and Cavalier of England—chivalry gentle always
and lowly, among those who deserved
their name of knight; showing mercy to
whom mercy was due, and honor to whom
honor."

See further the definition of a squire:
"first it means a rider; or, in more full
and perfect sense, a governor of beasts,
. . . which is the primal meaning of chiv-

alry, the horse, as the noblest, because trainablest, of wild creatures, being taken for a type of them all." And further (*Fors*, lxxv., p. 415), " And of all essential things in a gentleman's bodily and mental training, this is really the beginning— that he should have close companionship with the horse, the dog, and the eagle. Of all birthrights and bookrights—this is his first. He needn't be a Christian— there have been millions of Pagan gentlemen; he needn't be kind—there have been millions of cruel gentlemen; he needn't be honest—there have been millions of crafty gentlemen. He needn't know how to read, or to write his own name. But he *must* have horse, dog, and eagle for friends. If, then, he has also Man for his friend, he is a noble gentleman; and if God for his friend, a king. And if, being honest, being kind, and having God and Man for his friends, he *then* gets these three brutal friends, besides his angelic ones, he is perfect in earth, as for heaven. For, to be his friends, these must be brought up with him, and he with them. Falcon on fist, hound at foot, and horse part of himself—Eques, Ritter, Cavalier, Chevalier.

"Yes; horse and dog you understand the good of; but what's the good of the falcon, think you?

"To be friends with the falcon must mean that you love to see it soar; that is to say, you love fresh air and the fields."

Here we no doubt have love of the horse, and of animals, and of fresh air, and of exercise. But Mr. Ruskin will forgive me if I venture really to doubt whether it is not in the clothing of the mediæval palfrey that he actually loves the steed. I do not think that he in his heart loves the horse as a rider loves him. His words involuntarily make me believe that it is not the habit of mind formed by the boy whose taste for sport is bred in his early games with other boys in the open field; but it smacks of the nursery and the school-room, perhaps the garden; and the chase and the hunt have a flavor of the in-door dust which comes from the books on the shelf, with their accounts of the knight and the tourney. One who would measure sport by the exploits of the Knight, the Ritter, the Eques, the Cavalier, the Chevalier, can feel no sympathy (if he does not feel antipathy) with a modern gentleman in top-hat, breeches made by Tautz, and boots by Peel.

THE END

TENNYSON, RUSKIN, BROWNING.

Records of Tennyson, Ruskin, Browning. By Anne Thackeray Ritchie. Illustrated. Crown 8vo, Cloth, Ornamental, Uncut Edges and Gilt Top, $2 00.

The chapters comprised in this volume were written from the stand-point of personal recollections and appreciation, and not only present delightful glimpses of the home life and private characters of the famous persons to whom they relate, but afford many valuable and interesting comments upon their works, with estimates of their influence in the world of literature and of intellectual endeavor.

Partly personal, partly biographical, and wholly interesting and entertaining, the volume supplies the demand for a book which shall satisfy the legitimate interest in the lives and personalities of these great men.—*Philadelphia Inquirer.*

In many ways it affords the best information in regard to the personalities of these three modern masters that has been printed. Mrs. Ritchie had personal knowledge of them, and writes in full sympathy with their lives and works—*N. Y. Times.*

Published by HARPER & BROTHERS, New York.

☞ *The above works are for sale by all booksellers, or will be sent by the publishers, postage prepaid, to any part of the United States, Canada, or Mexico, on receipt of the price.*

HARPER'S AMERICAN ESSAYISTS.

16mo, Cloth, Ornamental, $1 00 each.

PICTURE AND TEXT. By HENRY JAMES. With Portrait and Illustrations.

AMERICANISMS AND BRITICISMS, With Other Essays on Other Isms. By BRANDER MATTHEWS. With Portrait.

FROM THE BOOKS OF LAURENCE HUTTON. With Portrait.

CONCERNING ALL OF US. By THOMAS WENT-WORTH HIGGINSON. With Portrait.

FROM THE EASY CHAIR. By GEORGE WILLIAM CURTIS. With Portrait.

OTHER ESSAYS FROM THE EASY CHAIR. By GEORGE WILLIAM CURTIS. With Portrait.

AS WE WERE SAYING. By CHARLES DUDLEY WARNER. With Portrait and Illustrations.

CRITICISM AND FICTION. By WILLIAM DEAN HOWELLS. With Portrait.

PUBLISHED BY HARPER & BROTHERS, NEW YORK.

☞ *The above works are for sale by all booksellers, or will be sent by the publishers, postage prepaid, to any part of the United States, Canada, or Mexico, on receipt of the price.*

By GEORGE WILLIAM CURTIS.

FROM THE EASY CHAIR. **With Portrait.** 16mo, **Cloth,** Ornamental, $1 00.

OTHER ESSAYS **FROM THE** EASY CHAIR. **With Portrait.** 16mo, Cloth, Ornamental, **$1** 00.

PRUE AND I. Illustrated Edition. **8vo,** Illuminated Silk, $3 50. **Also** 12mo, **Cloth,** Gilt Tops, $1 **50.**

LOTUS-EATING. **A** Summer **Book.** Illustrated **by** KENSETT. **12mo,** Cloth, Gilt Tops, **$1 50.**

NILE **NOTES OF A** HOWADJI. **12mo,** Cloth, Gilt Tops, $1 **50.**

THE HOWADJI IN SYRIA. 12mo, Cloth, Gilt **Tops, $1** 50.

THE POTIPHAR PAPERS. Illustrated by HOPPIN. 12mo, Cloth, Gilt Tops, **$1 50.**

TRUMPS. A Novel. Illustrated by **HOPPIN.** 12mo, Cloth, Gilt Tops, $1 **50.**

JAMES RUSSELL LOWELL. Illustrated. **16mo,** Cloth, Ornamental, 50 cents.

WENDELL PHILLIPS. **A** Eulogy. 8vo, Paper, **25 cents.**

PUBLISHED BY HARPER & BROTHERS, NEW YORK.

☞ *The **above works are for** sale by all booksellers, or will be sent by the publishers, postage prepaid. to any part of **the** United States, Canada, **or** Mexico, on receipt of the price.*